Srimati's Vegetarian Delights

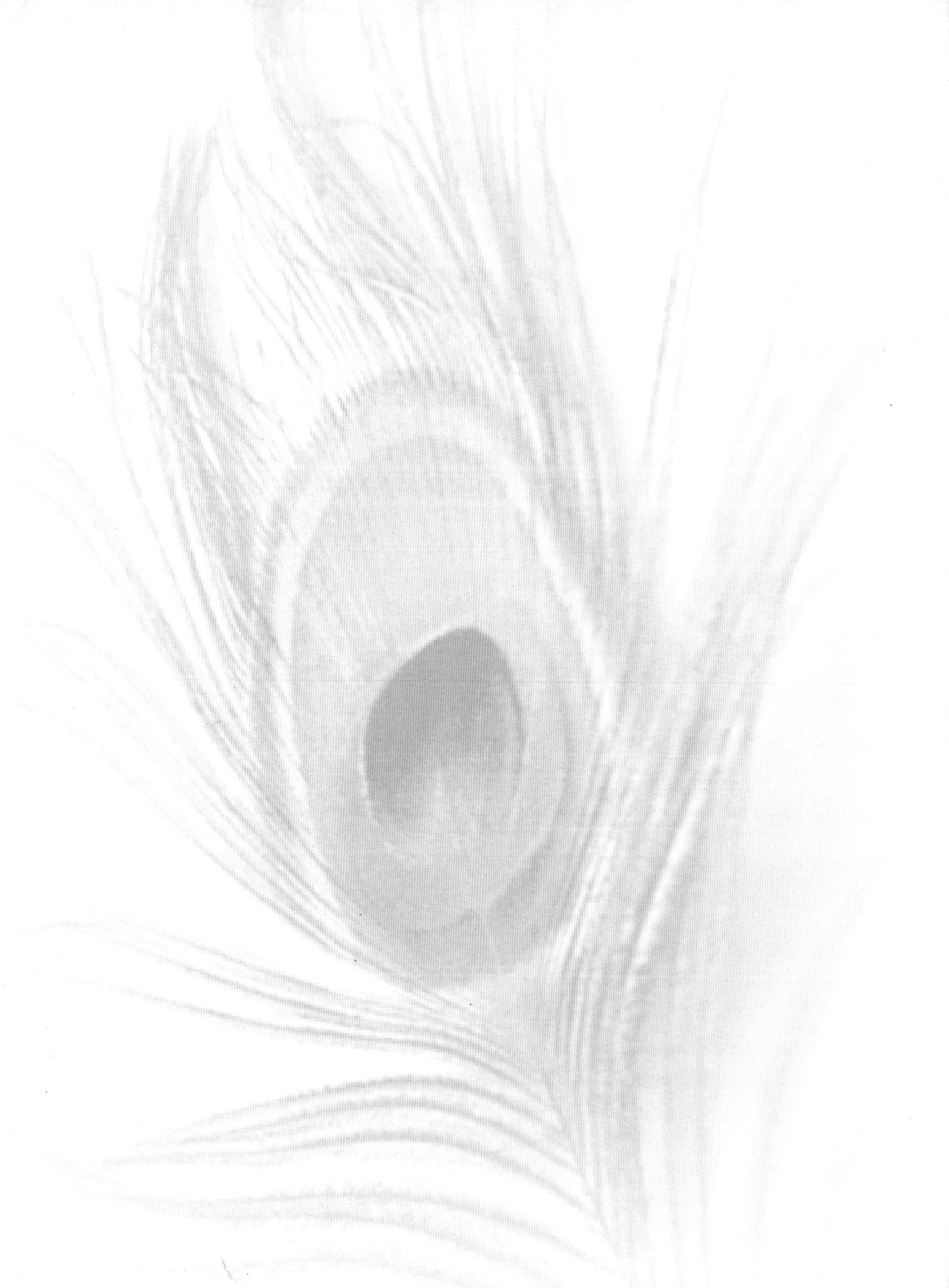

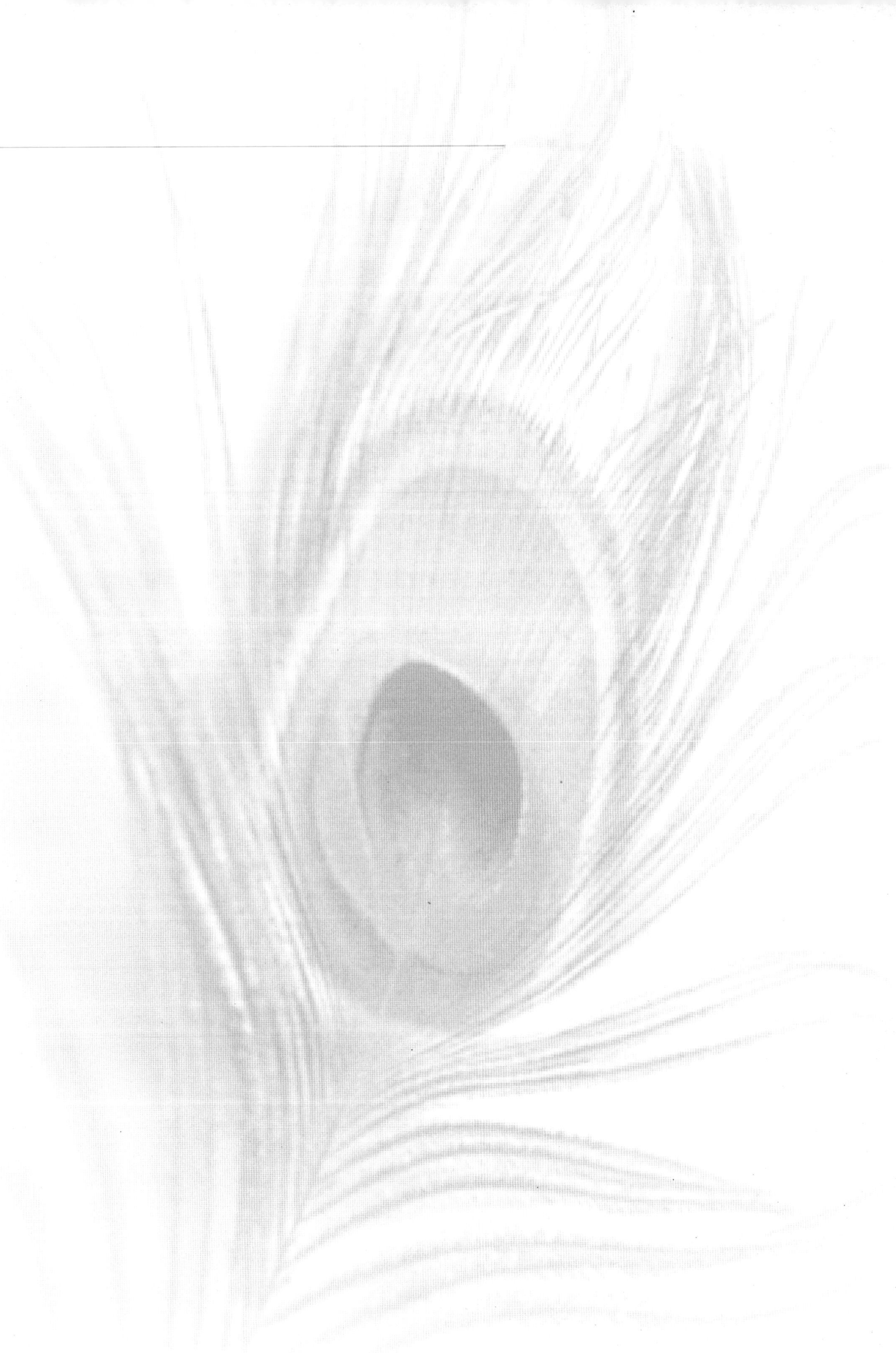

Text & Direction: Srimati Dasi
Photography: Srimati Dasi
Illustrations: Dhanishta Devi Dasi
Design & Concept: Ramesh Dwarika and Rakesh Sookun
Image Editing: Ramesh Dwarika and Rakesh Sookun
Cover Design by Isvara Dasa (Touchstone Media)

ISBN: 81-87897-27-9

Published by Touchstone Media 2011
www.touchstonemedia.com

Srimati's Vegetarian Delights

By Srimati Dasi

TOUCH STONE
MEDIA

Dedicated to
His Holiness Srila Giriraj Maharaja

Srila Prabhupada explains that in the material concept if you give something away, you loose it. But in spiritual life, the more you give the more you receive.

Whatever I have learnt and whatever experience I have gained in Krsna consciousness, I offer at your Divine Lotus feet and may I distribute it to others!

A special thanks to:

- To my dearest mother, Biddy Johnson, who has supported all my ambitions in life,
- to my father, Peter Johnson, for his contribution,
- to my beloved husband, Krishna dasa Kaviraja Dasa, for all his support and encouragement,
- to my children, Subadra and Balaram, for all their sweetness,
- to my sister, Ingrid Thomson, for editing,
- to Dhanistha Dasi for the art work,
- to Ramesh Dwarika and Rakesh Sookun for layout and design,
- to Davish Dookheet for the peacock picture,
- to Deven Thomson and Yves Bamani for assisting me with the computer,
- to Reena Sukdev for giving an enormous amount of her time helping me in so many ways,
- to Debbie Lamoral, Dhira Lalita Dasi, Claudia Steensma, Adele Joseph, Charles Johnson and to the staff at Nitai's Pure Vegetarian Snack for all their help and support,
- and to everyone who has contributed to the completion of this book.

contents

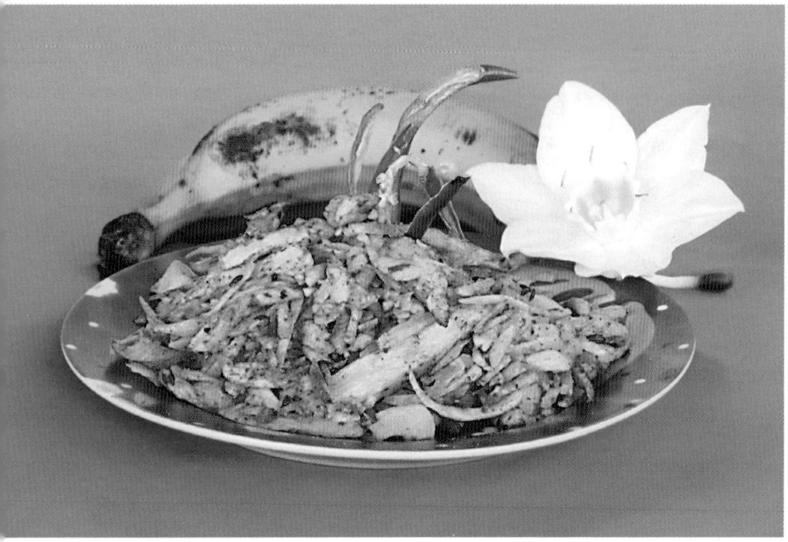

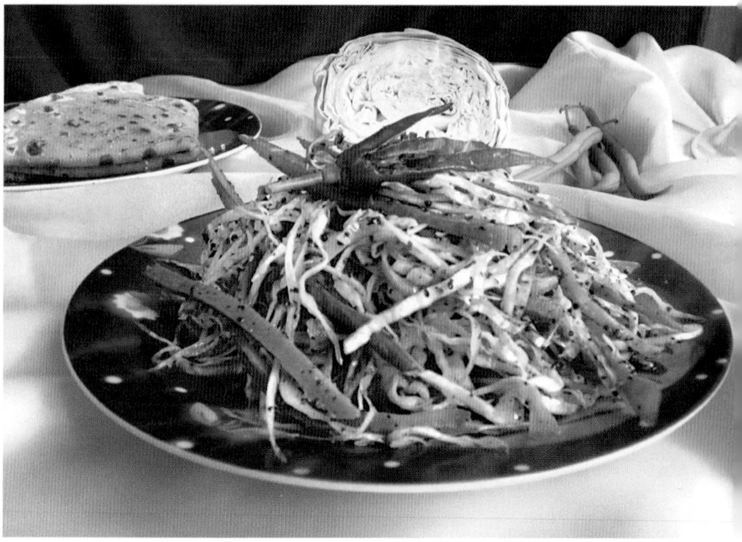

Contents

Contents

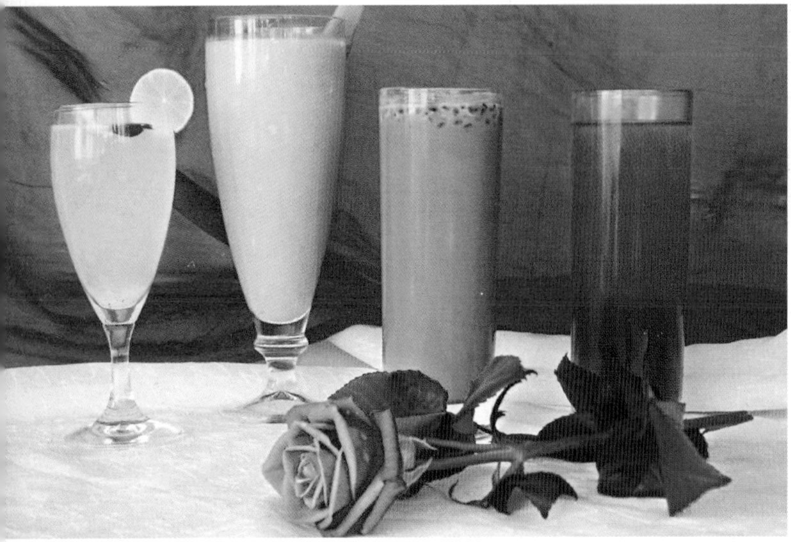

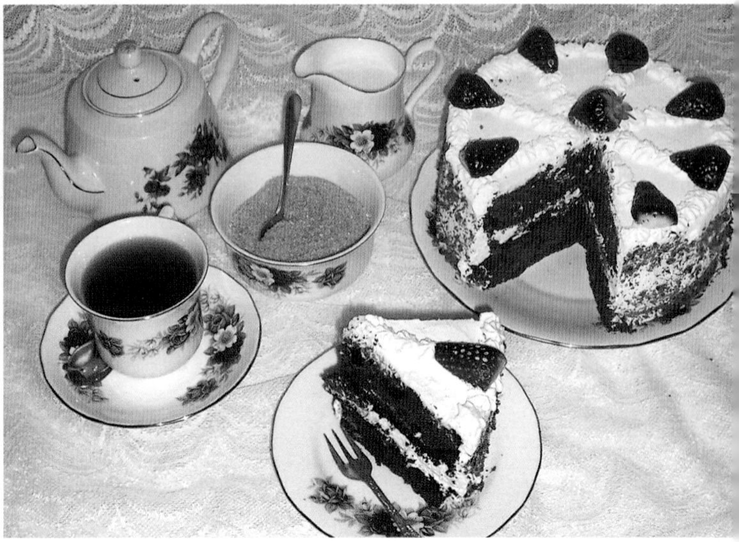

Contents

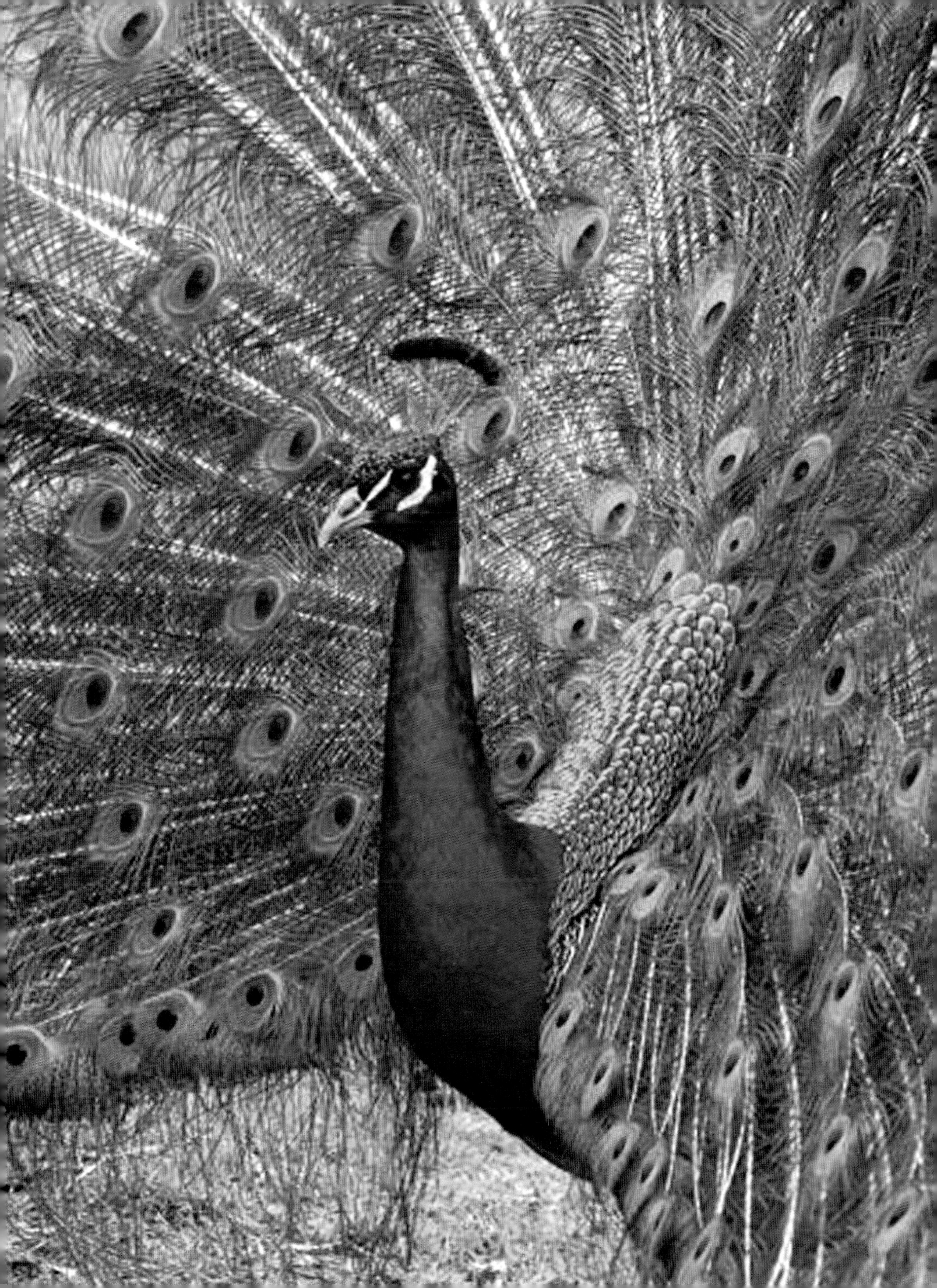

SPICES

1. Mint
2. Ginger
3. Chilies
4. Green mung dhal
5. Yellow pea dhal
6. Aniseed seeds
7. Mustard seeds
8. Fenugreek seeds
9. Cumin seeds
10. Ajwain seeds
11. Cardamom pods
12. Cloves
13. Cinnamon sticks
14. Masala/Curry powder
15. Tumeric powder

INTRODUCTION

$\mathcal{V}$egetarianism is becoming more popular as many people are adopting a more holistic approach to life. Part of today's trend is also the acceptance of other cultures and traditions and as a result, a natural blending of cultures is occurring. We can see this in the kitchen as oriental spices are being used more in the Western homes and Asians are becoming more exposed to the Western cuisine and style of dining.

My experience has allowed me the opportunity to produce a wonderful blend of classical infusions from both the Eastern and Western worlds. The aim is to promote pure vegetarian cooking to help bridge the cultural gaps, leading towards a peaceful society.

FOOD FOR THE SOUL

The Vedic scriptures of India teach basic human values, which have moulded my life as a vegetarian.

In Bhagavad Gita Lord Krishna says that if you offer Him with love and devotion a leaf, a flower, a fruit or water He will accept it (Bag Gita, Ch9, Text 26):

patram puspam phalamtoyam
yo me bhaktya ptayaccati
tad aham bhakty - upahrtam
asnami prayatmanah

He does not ask for meat, fish or eggs so we can not offer Him these foods, if we do, that will not be considered love.

Followers of Vedic tradition do not cook with onion and garlic because these are considered foods in the modes of passion (also known as rajasic foods). Such foods are too bitter, sour, salty, hot, pungent, dry and burning (Bag Gita, Ch.17, Text 9):

katv-amla-lavanaty-usna-
tiksna-ruksa-vidahinah
ahara rajasasyesta
duhkha-sokamaya-pradah

By eating such foods ones behavior will also be affected.

Bhagavad Gita further explains that foods in the mode of ignorance (also known as tamasic foods), are foods that are tasteless, decomposed, putrid, consists of remnants and untouchable things such as meat, fish and eggs and should be avoided completely (Bag Gita, Ch 17, Text 10):

yata-yamam gata-rasam
puti paryusitam ca yat
ucchistam api camedhyam
bhojanam tamada-priyam

Then, there are foods in the mode of goodness (also known as sattvic foods), which increase the duration of life, purify ones existence, give strength, health, happiness and satisfaction. They are juicy, fatty, wholesome and pleasing to the heart (Bag Gita, Ch 17, Text 8):

ayuh sattva-balarogya-
sukha-priti-vivardhanah
rasyah snigdhah sthira hrdya
aharah sattvika-priyah

Such foods are desired. Milk, fruit, vegetables and grains fall into this category.

If one wants to be peaceful, one must eat peacefully. This can be achieved by eating foods in the mode of goodness. Consuming violent diets where innocent animals are slaughtered will contradict ones efforts to be peaceful.

KARMA-FREE FOOD

One may argue that plants also have life and is one not incurring sin by consuming them?

The Vedic scriptures explain that one living entity is food for another. Cheetahs have sharp canines and long claws meant for catching prey but they attack only when they are hungry. Humans have no claws and sharp teeth to attack animals. We have to rely on artificial means to have meat everyday, making the diet unnatural. One does take life from vegetables and fruit but they do not have nervous systems to perceive pain, which makes the reaction minimal. One should offer ones food to God so that it becomes karma-free, which means there will be no reactions.

TYPES OF VEGETARIANS

There are three main categories of vegetarians, lacto-ova vegetarians, lacto vegetarians and vegan.

LACTO-OVA VEGETARIANS
Lacto-ova vegetarians consume eggs and dairy products. They do not include meat, poultry or fish in their diet.

LACTO VEGETARIANS
Lacto vegetarians consume dairy products but no meat, poultry, fish or eggs. One reason for not consuming eggs could be that the egg once had the ability to produce life. Milk is used because the cow is considered like the mother as she gives abundance of milk, more that her calf can drink.

VEGANS
Vegans do not consume meat, poultry, fish, eggs or dairy products. Some people may not agree as to how the cows are treated in the dairy farms so they do not want to use dairy products. Lactose intolerance could be another reason why people do not use milk products.

All vegetarians can use this recipe book. Vegans can find many suitable recipes. Fresh cow's milk can always be replaced by soya milk and curd can be substituted by tofu derived from soya milk.

WHEAT-FREE DIETS
There are recipes that are suitable for a wheat-free diet such as the non-grain pancakes, non-grain pooris and sago and potato patties.

EKADASI
For those who follow Ekadasi, a day of fasting from grains and beans, wheat-free dishes can be used. Some dishes may need to be adjusted by omitting mustard seeds and hing. Commercial ground spices should also be avoided as often rice flour is added.

A BALANCED DIET

To maintain good health, everyone needs exercise, fresh air and a balanced diet. The basic principle of good nutrition is to include foods that help one grow, go and glow.

A vegetarian can achieve a balanced diet by making sure he or she has enough protein from food sources such as lentils, dhals, beans and soya products. Soya milk products should be taken if no dairy products are consumed. Include lots of fruit and vegetables for vitamins and mineral and enough fats and oils in the body.

PROTEIN
Protein is needed for growth, repairing tissues and protection against infections. There are twenty-two essential amino acids (components of protein). Eight of them are essential in an adult's diet and can only be acquired by consuming certain foods that contain these components. All the necessary amino acids can be obtained by combining foods such as rice and legumes; rice and sesame seeds; beans and milk; wholewheat products and milk.

IRON
Iron is essential for making haemoglobin, which carries the oxygen around the body and is needed to prevent anemia. Green leafy vegetables, beans, nuts, wholewheat grain, raisins and apricots contain iron. Food rich in vitamin C (fresh vegetables and citrus fruit) should be consumed so that iron can be absorbed in the body.

VITAMIN B12
A small amount of vitamin B12 is needed for growth, production of red blood cells and a healthy nervous system. This vitamin is mainly found in animal foods so if one consumes dairy products, one need not worry. Vitamin B12 is commercially produced from a fungus and is found in many foods that are fortified. Soya beans, wheat-germ, whole grains and brewers yeast also contain this vitamin.

CALCIUM
Calcium is needed for bone and tooth formation, blood clotting, muscle function, nerve transmission and blood pressure. Ones calcium needs will be met if one consumes dairy products. Calcium is also available in dark green leafy vegetables, broccoli, legumes, tofu, walnuts and sunflower seeds.

OMEGA 3 AND 6 OILS
Flaxseed, evening primrose oil and walnuts are a good source of omega 3 and 6 oils for a vegetarian.

MEASUREMENT AND TEMPERATURE GUIDE

METRIC MEASUREMENTS

¼ teaspoon	1,2 ml
½ teaspoon	2,5 ml
1 teaspoon	5 ml
2 teaspoons	10 ml
3 teaspoons	15 ml
¼ cup	60 ml
½ cup	125 ml
¾ cup	180 ml
1 cup	250 ml
2 cups	500 ml
3 cups	750 ml
4 cups	1000 ml or 1 litre

OVEN TEMPERATURES

°F	°C	Gas	Oven
200	100		
250	120	¼ - ½	Very cool
275	140		
300	150	1	Cool
325	160	2	Moderate cool
350	180	3	Moderate
375	190	4	Moderately hot
400	200		Hot
425	220	5	Very hot
450	230	6	Extremely hot
500	260	7 - 8	

ABBREVIATIONS

g	gram
ml	millilitre
cm	centimetre
mm	millimetre
°F	degree Fahrenheit
°C	degree Celsius

UTENSILS

Cooking utensils can vary from culture to culture. An inexperienced cook might not be familiar with the type of utensils used in a cookbook.
Having had the opportunity to cook in both Eastern and Western homes, I have chosen to use the more modern equivalents. For example, in India spices are usually ground with a mortar and pestle but can be equally and efficiently ground in an electrical coffee grinder. Similarly, chutneys are usually crushed on a rock but can be blended in a food processor.

Use standard measuring utensils such as measuring cups, spoons and a kitchen scale for weighing vegetables.

THESE ARE SOME OF THE UTENSILS YOU

WILL NEED
- A set of measuring spoons and cups
- A kitchen scale
- A chopping board and knife
- A rolling pin
- A large ladle with holes
- A colander
- Different sized mixing bowls
- Heavy-based stainless steel saucepans
- A saucepan for deep-frying (or a karhai, which is a deep heavy-based metal wok)
- A wok for stir-frying
- A small pressure-cooker
- A griddle pan (also known as a tava)

MAKING YOGHURT

Homemade yoghurt has a very pleasant taste and is easy to digest. Yoghurt can be used in many preparations such as salad dressings and fruit lassies. A starter culture, which can be unsweetened commercial yoghurt, is needed to start the yoghurt making process.

1 litre full cream milk
¼ cup (60 ml) yoghurt starter culture
2 tbs (30 ml) milk powder (optional)

Boil the milk and then allow it cool down to about 48° C or 118° F (the temperature of the warmth of a bottle of milk one would use for a baby). Whisk in the yoghurt culture and milk powder.

- Cover and wrap in a large cloth and place in a warm area, undisturbed, for at least 6 hours or overnight. The bacteria in the culture will grow and transform the milk into thick yoghurt.

As there will be no extra-added preservatives the yoghurt will only last up to three days under refrigeration.

MAKING FRESH HOMEMADE CHEESE (CURD)

When milk sours it separates into curds and whey. The curd is the solid part of the milk and is rich in protein while the whey is the liquid part. In the Indian cuisine curd is known as panir and forms the basis of many dishes such as Matar Panir, Palak Panir, Malai Panir and Ras Malai.

Soya milk can be separated in a similar manner to form tofu. All the curd recipes in this book can be replaced by tofu if one is a vegan. For example, the cheese cake recipe can be made with tofu instead of curd.

The quality of milk one uses will determine the quantity of curd yield. For this reason, I have given the weight measurement for all the curd recipes.
Preferably use a rich full cream cows milk when making curd.

⅓
Curd can be kept for three days in the refrigerator or stored in the freezer and defrosted when needed. The remaining whey can be kept for adding to soups, dhals and stews.

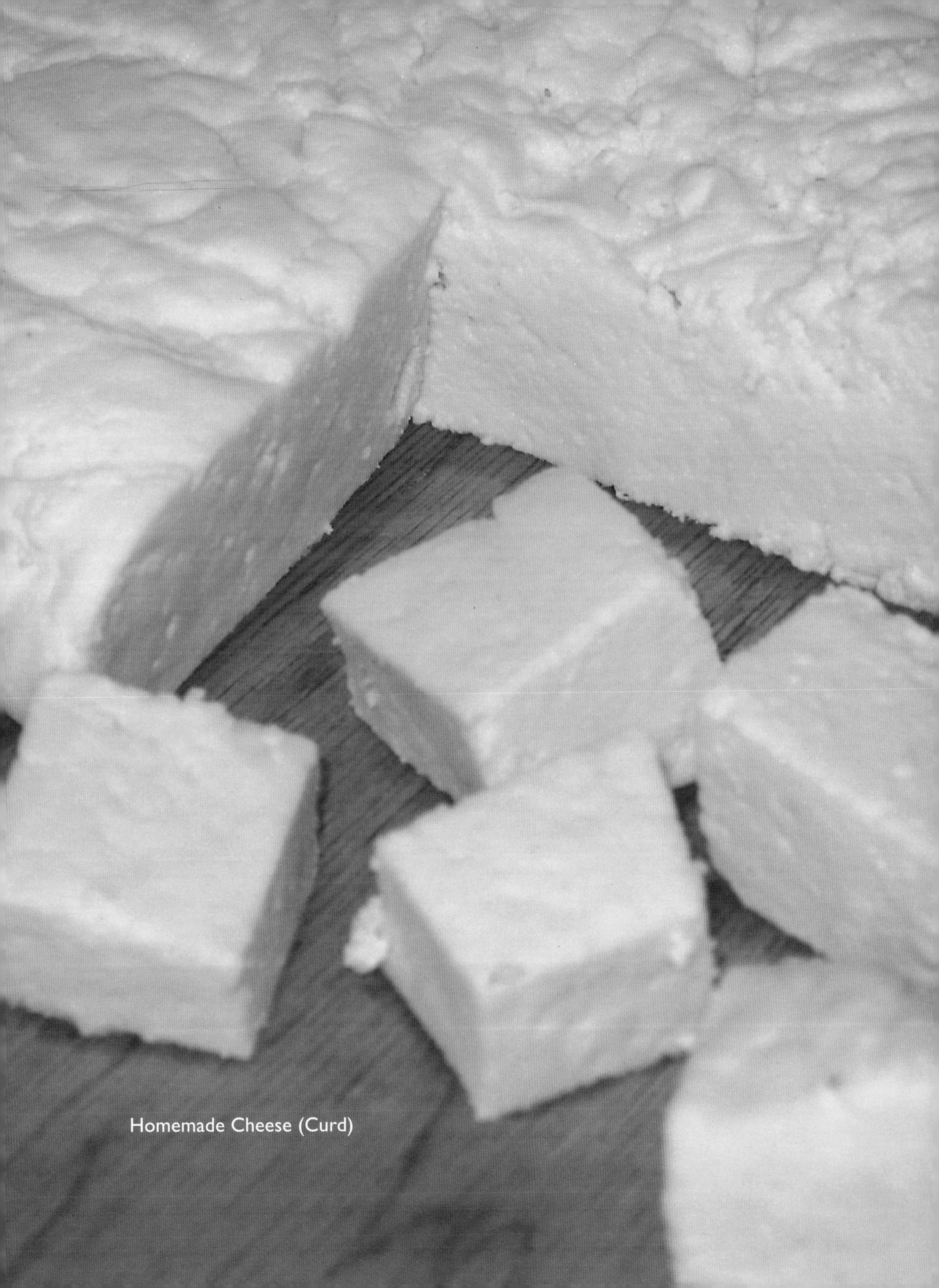

Homemade Cheese (Curd)

South Indian Dhal (Rasam)

Soups and Dhals

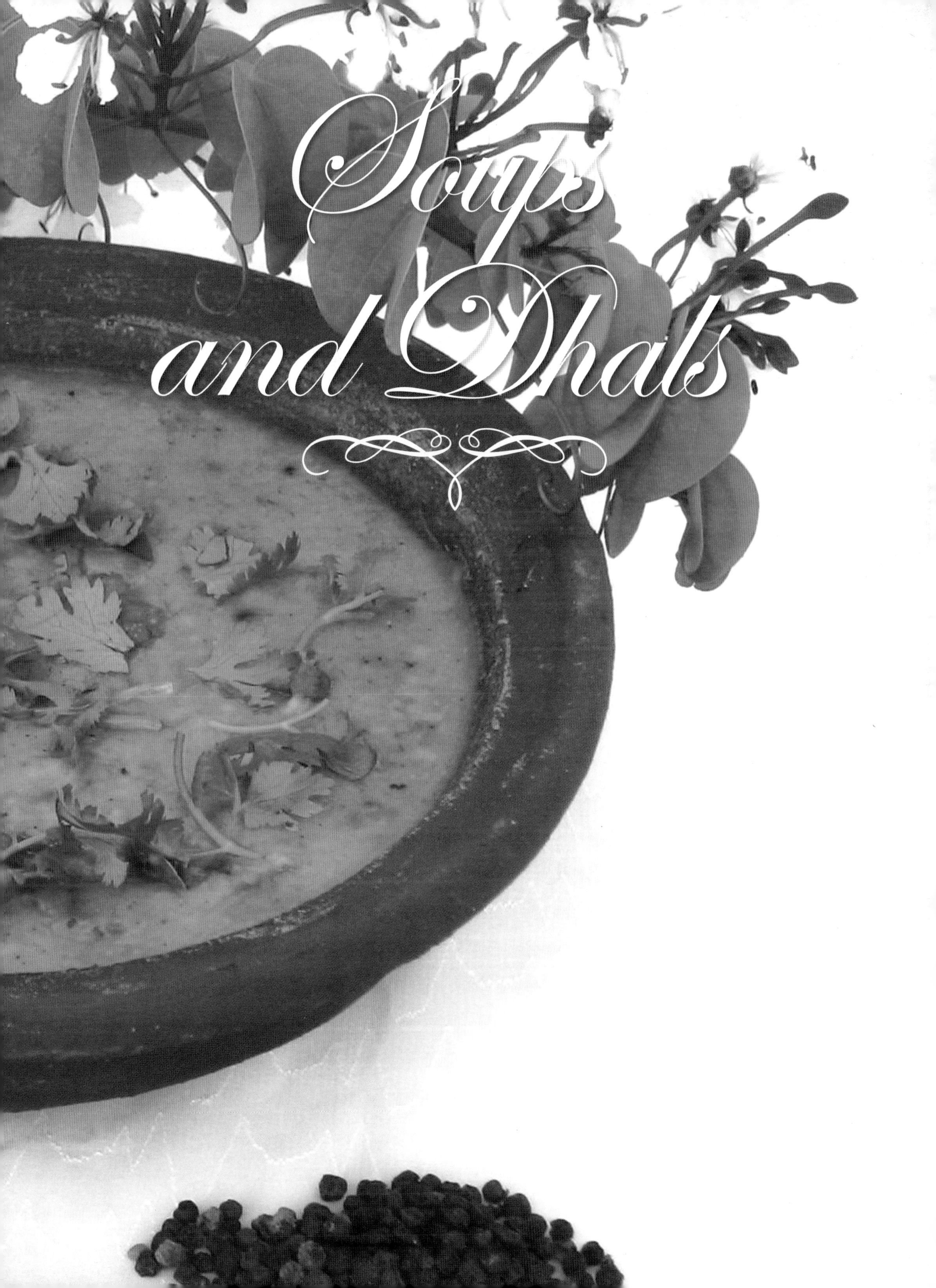

Baby Potato Consommé

An attractive way to serve baby potatoes as a starter.

Preparation time : 30 minutes
Serves : 4 - 6 persons

1 tbs (15 ml) butter
1 tsp (5 ml) finely grated ginger
½ tsp (2,5 ml) hing
1 medium tomato finely diced (optional)
4 cups (1000 ml) water
2 tsp (10 ml) salt
10 baby potatoes (approx 460g) rinsed and sliced into thin rounds
1 tbs (15 ml) finely chopped fresh coriander or parsley

- Melt the butter in a medium-sized saucepan.
- Add the ginger, hing and tomato. Sauté until soft and velvety.
- Stir in the water and salt. Bring to boil.
- Fold in the potatoes and allow to simmer for about 20 minutes or until the potatoes are well cooked.
- Garnish with coriander or parsley.

Chinese Cabbage Consommé

Transparent soup made with Chinese cabbage (Tein Jin).

Preparation time : 20 minutes
Serves : 4 - 6 persons

1 tbs (15 ml) oil
1 tsp (5 ml) finely grated ginger
½ tsp (2,5 ml) hing
1 medium tomato finely diced
4 cups (1000 ml) water
1 tsp (5 ml) salt
1 finely shredded Chinese cabbage (approx 175 - 200 g)

- Heat the oil in a medium-sized saucepan.
- Add ginger and hing followed by the tomato and sauté until soft and velvety.
- Stir in the water and salt. Bring to a gentle boil.
- Add the lettuce and allow to simmer for about ten minutes.

* *Variation : Use watercress in place of Chinese cabbage.*

Cream of Butternut Soup

A creamy butternut soup that is light and tasty.

Preparation time : 20 - 25 minutes
Serves : 4 - 6 persons

*1 medium butternut (approx 350 g) peeled, seeded
and cut into chunks*
2 tbs (30 ml) butter
¼ tsp (1,2 ml) nutmeg
¼ tsp (1,2 ml) hing
¼ tsp (1,2 ml) black pepper
1 ½ cups (375 ml) milk
1 tsp (5 ml) salt
2 tbs (30 ml) fresh cream
1 tbs (15 ml) finely chopped parsley

• Steam the butternut until soft and then mash.
• Melt the butter in a medium-sized saucepan.
• Add the nutmeg, hing and black pepper.
• Whisk in the milk and salt. Bring to a gentle boil.
• Allow to simmer for 10 - 15 minutes.
• Serve in individual bowls garnished with cream
  and parsley.

* *Variations: Use pumpkin or asparagus in place of
  butternut.*

Cream of Corn Soup

A delightful soup with a touch of oriental flavour.

Preparation time : 20 minutes
Serves : 4 - 6 persons

*1 cup (250 ml) freshly boiled or frozen
corn kernels*
2 cups (500 ml) milk
½ tsp (2,5 ml) ground coriander
½ tsp (2,5 ml) ground cumin
½ tsp (2,5 ml) ground fennel
¼ tsp (1,2 ml) hing
¼ tsp (1,2 ml) black pepper
1 tsp (5 ml) salt
1 tbs (15 ml) butter
2 tbs (30 ml) fresh cream
1 tbs (15 ml) finely chopped parsley

• Grind the corn into a smooth paste using a food
  processor. Add a little of the milk if necessary.
• In a medium-sized saucepan whisk the corn,
  milk, spices and seasoning together and bring
  to a gentle boil.
• Add the butter and allow to simmer for
  5 minutes.
• Just before serving garnish with cream
  and parsley.

SOUPS & DHALS

Hearty Vegetable Soup
A thick winter soup with vegetables and noodles.

Preparation time : 50 minutes
Serves : 6 - 8 persons

I medium potato peeled and diced into small cubes
I small carrot diced into small cubes
¼ cup (60 ml) small cauliflower florets
¼ cup (60 ml) finely shredded cabbage
¼ cup (60 ml) chopped green beans
¼ cup (60 ml) fresh corn kernels
I sprig of celery
I medium tomato blanched
and puréed
½ tsp (2,5 ml) black pepper
I tsp (5 ml) oregano
¼ tsp (1,2 ml) hing
I tsp (5 ml) salt
4 cups (1000 ml) water
I tbs (15 ml) butter

½ cup (125 ml) pasta broken
into pieces
¼ cup (60 ml) fresh or frozen
green peas
I tbs (15 ml) finely chopped
parsley

- Place all the ingredients in a pressure-cooker except for the pasta and the green peas if using frozen. Cook for 30 minutes.
- Remove the lid and add the pasta. Simmer for a further 15 minutes or until the pasta is tender.
- Towards the end of the cooking add the frozen green peas.
- Garnish with parsley.

Chickpea Dhal with Eggplant
Eggplant sliced into long strips makes this dhal unique.

Preparation time : 30 minutes
Serves : 4 - 6 persons

Step One
I cup (250 ml) chickpea dhal soaked overnight, then
drained
I ½ tsp (7,5 ml) salt
½ tsp (2,5 ml) oil or ghee
4 cups (1000 ml) water
I medium eggplant cut into half and then into
long strips

I chili finely chopped
6 - 8 curry leaves
I tsp (5 ml) turmeric powder
¼ tsp (1,2 ml) hing
I medium tomato finely diced
I tbs (15 ml) finely chopped fresh coriander

- Pressure-cook the dhal, salt, oil or ghee and water for 15 to 20 minutes.
- Halfway through the cooking, add the eggplant.

Step Two
I tbs (15 ml) oil or ghee
½ tsp (2,5 ml) mustard seeds
½ tsp (2,5 ml) cumin seeds

- Heat the oil or ghee in a small saucepan.
- Add the mustard seeds and when they begin to splutter, add the cumin seeds, chili and curry leaves followed by turmeric powder and hing.
- Add the tomato and sauté until soft and velvety.
- Fold into the dhal and simmer for about two minutes.
- Garnish with coriander.

Mung Dhal with Zuccini and Carrots

A wholesome dhal soup with vegetables.

Preparation time : 30 minutes
Serves : 4 - 6 persons

1 cup (250 ml) mung dhal soaked overnight,
then drained
1 medium zucchini cut into thin rounds
1 medium carrot cut into thin rounds
4 cups (1000 ml) water
1 tsp (5 ml) salt
1 tbs (15 ml) oil or ghee
½ tsp (2,5 ml) mustard seeds
½ tsp (2,5 ml) cumin seeds
1 chili finely chopped
1 sprig of thyme
1 tsp (5 ml) turmeric powder
¼ tsp (1,2 ml) hing
1 medium tomato finely diced
1 tbs (15 ml) finely chopped fresh coriander

- Pressure-cook the dhal, zucchini, carrots, water, salt and ½ teaspoon (2,5 ml) of the oil or ghee for 15 - 20 minutes.
- Heat the remaining oil or ghee in a small saucepan.
- Add the mustard seeds and when they begin to splutter, add the cumin seeds, chili and thyme followed by the turmeric powder and hing.
- Add the tomato and sauté until soft and velvety.
- Fold into the dhal and simmer for about 2 minutes.
- Garnish with coriander.

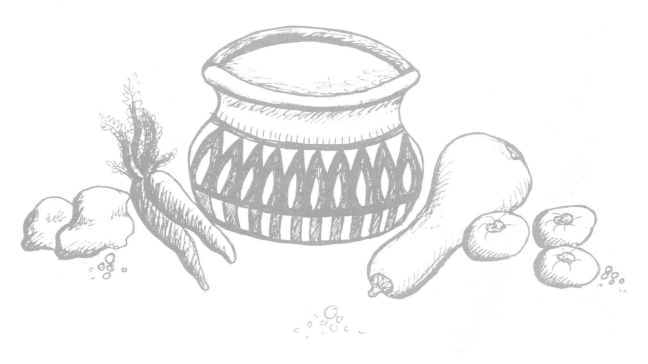

Mung Dhal with Zucchini and Carrots

South Indian Dhal (Rasam)

A fiery and spicy soup.

Preparation time : 30 minutes
Serves : 4 - 6 persons

Step One

1 cup (250 ml) toor dhal or yellow split pea dhal
soaked overnight, then drained
4 cups (1000 ml) water
1 tsp (5 ml) oil or ghee
1 ½ tsp (7,5 ml) salt

• Pressure-cook all the ingredients
  for 15 - 20 minutes.

Step Two

1 tsp (5 ml) mustard seeds
1 tsp (5 ml) cumin seeds
1 tsp (5 ml) coriander seeds
¼ tsp (1,2 ml) fenugreek
4 black pepper corns

• Dry roast the spices in a pan, then grind into
  a fine powder.

Step Three

1 tbs (15 ml) oil or ghee
6 - 8 curry leaves
1 chili finely chopped
¼ tsp (1,2 ml) hing
1 tsp (5 ml) turmeric powder
1 medium tomato finely diced
1 tbs (15 ml) tamarind pulp
½ cup (125 ml) water
1 tbs (15 ml) finely chopped fresh coriander

• Heat the oil or ghee in a medium-sized saucepan.
• Add the curry leaves and chili followed by the
  hing and turmeric powder.
• Add the tomato and sauté until soft and velvety.
• Fold in the ground spices (as prepared in step
  two) and dhal.
• Soak the tamarind in the ½ cup (125 ml) water
  and strain from pips.
• Mix the tamarind water into the dhal and simmer
  for 5 minutes.
• Garnish with coriander.

* *Variation : Before pressure-cooking the dhal,*
  add a small amount of vegetables such as carrots
  and green beans.

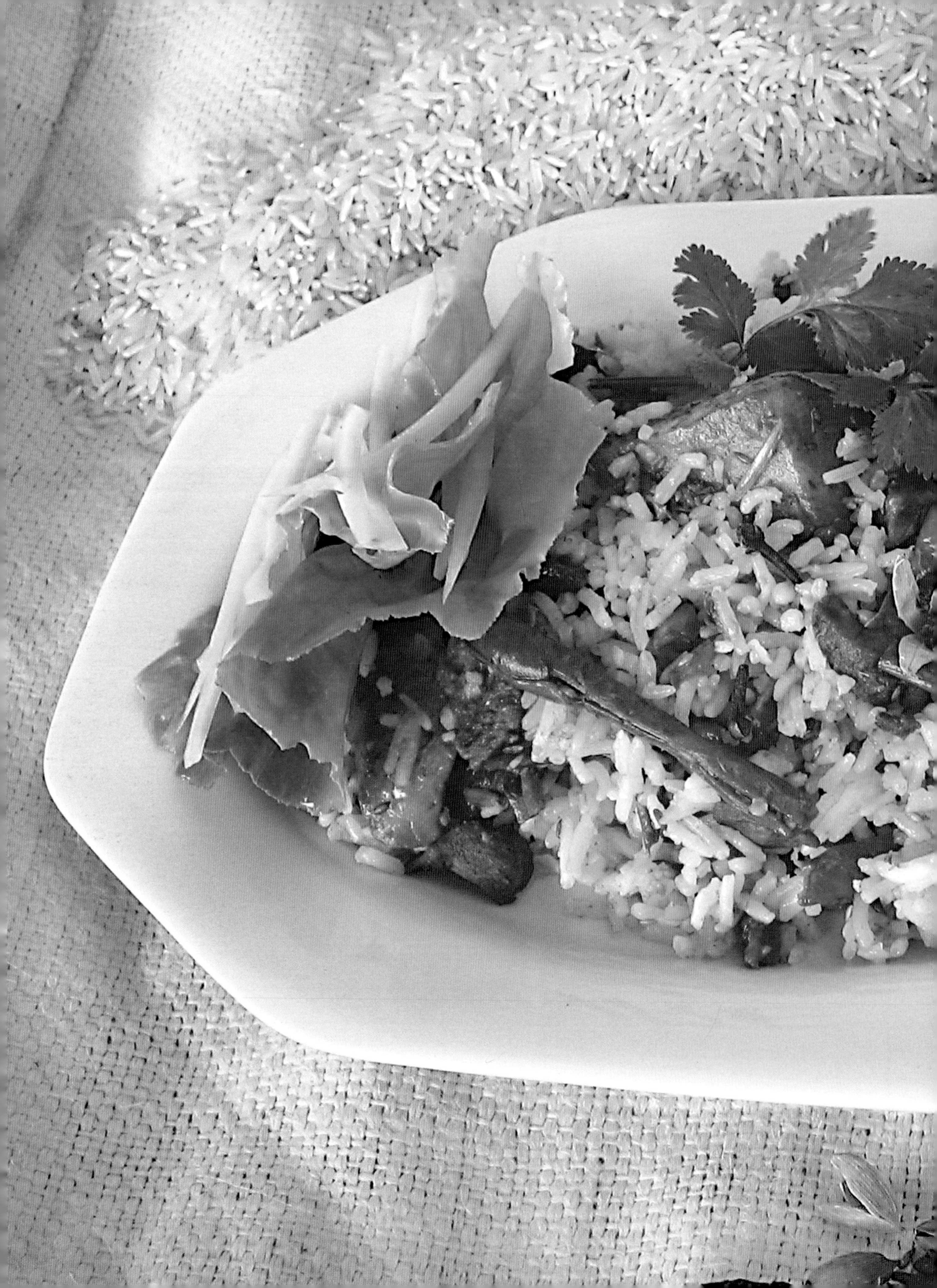

Rice dishes

Vegetable Rice (Biryani)

Basmati Rice

Basmati rice is far more nutritious and easier to digest than parboiled rice.
This recipe provides a simple way to cook rice.

Preparation time : 20 minutes
Serves : 4 - 6 persons

4 cups (1000 ml) water
½ tsp (2,5 ml) salt
1 tsp (5 ml) oil or ghee
½ tsp (2,5 ml) hing
2 cups (500 ml) basmati rice

• Bring the water, salt, oil or ghee and hing to
  a gentle boil in a medium- sized saucepan.

• Add the rice, stir once, cover and simmer over
  a low heat for about 12 minutes until all the water
  is absorbed and the rice grains are fluffy and white.
• Remove the lid and gently toss with a fork.

Serving suggestion: Simple white basmati rice can
accompany most vegetable dishes or can be used
as a base for stir-fried rice.

Carrot and Corn Rice

A light rice to serve as an accompaniment to a meal.

Preparation time : 20 minutes
Serves : 4 - 6 persons

1 tbs (15 ml) oil or ghee
¼ tsp (1,2 ml) mustard seeds
2 opened cardamom pods
1 cinnamon stick (approx 2 cm)
½ cup (125 ml) grated carrots
⅓ cup (80 ml) fresh or frozen corn kernels
2 cups (500 ml) basmati rice
4 cups (1000 ml) boiling water
½ tsp (2,5 ml) salt
¼ tsp (1,2 ml) hing

• Heat the oil or ghee in a medium-sized saucepan.
• Add the mustard seeds and when they begin to
  splutter, add the cardamom and cinnamon stick.
• Stir in the carrots, corn and rice. Sauté for a few
  moments.
• Add the boiling water, salt and hing.
• Stir once and cover. Simmer over a low heat for
  about 12 minutes until all the water is absorbed
  and the rice grains are fluffy and white.
• Gently toss with a fork.

Spinach Rice

An attractive rice dish with spinach.

Preparation time : 20 minutes
Serves : 4 - 6 persons

1 tbs (15 ml) oil or ghee
1 red dried chili (optional)
1 bunch spinach (approx 115 g) finely chopped
¼ tsp (1,2 ml) hing
2 cups (500 ml) basmati rice
4 cups (1000 ml) boiling water
1 tsp (5 ml) salt
Lemon wedges for garnishing

• Heat the oil or ghee in a medium-sized saucepan.
• Add the chili, spinach and hing. Sauté for
  a few moments.
• Add the rice, boiling water and salt.
• Stir once, cover and gently simmer over a low
  heat for about 12 minutes until all the water is
  absorbed and the rice grains are fluffy and white.
• Gently toss with a fork and garnish with
  lemon wedges.

Lemon Rice

A pleasant rice dish with the zest of lemon.

Preparation time : 20 minutes
Serves : 4 - 6 persons

1 tbs (15 ml) oil or ghee
½ tsp (2,5 ml) mustard seeds
1 cinnamon stick (approx 5 cm)
2 opened cardamom pods
¼ tsp (1,2 ml) hing
¼ tsp (1,2 ml) turmeric powder
4 cups (1000 ml) water
½ tsp (2,5 ml) salt
2 cups (500 ml) basmati rice
The juice and zest of 1 small lemon
1 tbs (15 ml) finely chopped fresh coriander

• Heat the oil or ghee in a medium-sized saucepan.
• Add the mustard seeds and when they begin to splutter, add the cinnamon stick, cardamom, hing and turmeric powder.
• Add the water and salt. Bring to a gentle boil.
• Stir in the rice, cover and simmer over low heat for about 12 minutes until all the water is absorbed and the rice grains are fluffy and white.
• Gently fold in the lemon juice and zest.
• Garnish with coriander.

Stir-fried Rice

A tasty rice dish with lots of vegetables and nuts.

Preparation time : 45 minutes
Serves : 4 - 6 persons

Step One: Precooking the rice
4 cups (1000 ml) water
1 tsp (5 ml) salt
1 tsp (5 ml) oil or ghee
2 cups (500 ml) basmati rice

• Bring the water, salt and oil or ghee to a gentle boil. Add the rice.
• Stir once, cover and simmer over low heat for 12 minutes until all the water is absorbed and the rice grains are fluffy and white.

Step Two: Preparing the spices and vegetables, then assembling
½ cup (125 ml) soya chunks
2 medium potatoes (approx 230 g) peeled and cut into thin chips
2 tbs (30 ml) olive oil
1 chili finely chopped
6 - 8 curry leaves
1 tsp (5 ml) finely grated ginger
½ tsp (2,5 ml) hing
1 cup (250 ml) or 50 g finely shredded cabbage
1 cup (250 ml) or 100 g green beans cut into long thin strips

2 medium carrots (approx 100 g) cut into long thin strips
1 small broccoli (approx 200 g) cut into small florets
⅓ cup (80 ml) freshy boiled or frozen corn kernels
⅓ cup (80 ml) freshly boiled or frozen green peas
⅓ cup (80 ml) roasted peanuts
4 tbs (60 ml) soy sauce
1 tbs (15 ml) finely chopped fresh coriander

• Boil the soya chunks until soft. Drain and squeeze out the excess water. Cut into small pieces and deep-fry until golden brown and crisp.
• Deep-fry the potato chips until golden brown.
• Heat the olive oil in a large wok. Add the chili, curry leaves and ginger. Fry for a few moments.
• Add the hing and cabbage followed by the beans, carrots and broccoli. Stir-fry until the vegetables are soft yet crisp.
• Toss in the potato chips, soya, corn, green peas, nuts, rice and soy sauce.
• Garnish with coriander.

Serving suggestion: Serve with coconut or peanut chutney.

Saffran Rice with Green Peas and Cashews

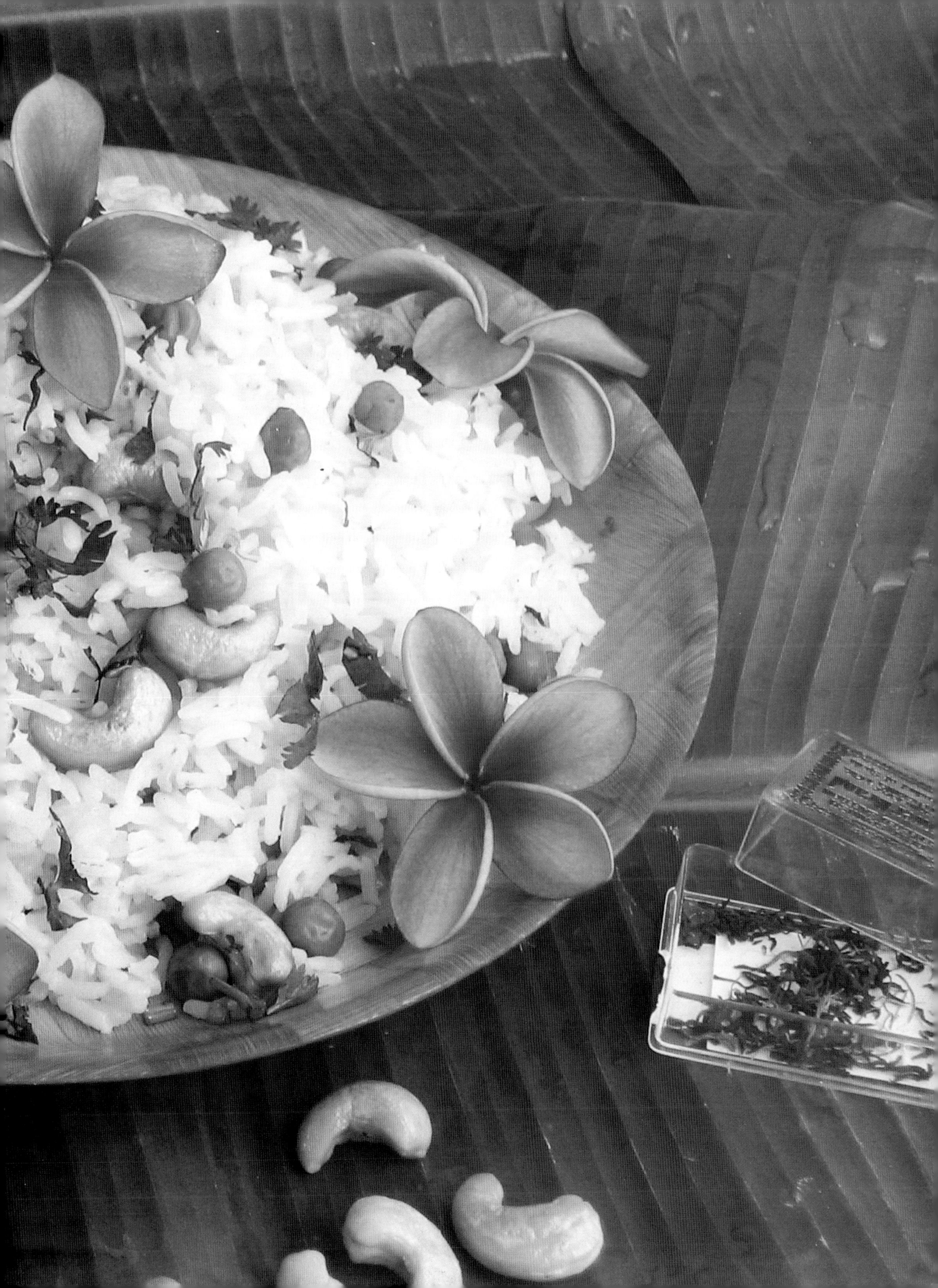

Saffron Rice with Green Peas and Cashews
An elegant rice dish for a special occasion.

1 tbs (15 ml) oil or ghee
½ cup (125 ml) cashew nuts
2 cups (500 ml) basmati rice
3 ¾ cups (930 ml) boiling water
½ tsp (2,5 ml) salt
¼ tsp (1,2 ml) hing
1 tsp (5 ml) saffron threads infused in ¼ cup
(60 ml) milk or water
½ cup (125 ml) freshly boiled or frozen green peas
1 tbs (15 ml) finely chopped fresh coriander

- Heat the oil or ghee in a medium-sized saucepan.
- Add the cashew nuts and braise for a few moments until golden brown.
- Add the rice, boiling water, salt, hing and saffron.
- Stir once, then add the green peas.
- Cover and simmer over a low heat for about 12 minutes until all the water is absorbed and the rice grains are fluffy and white.
- Gently toss with a fork.
- Garnish with coriander.

Savoury Rice (Pilau)
A rice dish with mixed vegetables.

Preparation time : 30 minutes
Serves : 4 - 6 persons

1 tbs (15 ml) oil or ghee
¼ tsp (1,2 ml) cumin seeds
1 cinnamon stick (approx 5 cm)
2 opened cardamom pods
4 whole black pepper corns
½ tsp (2,5 ml) turmeric powder
¼ tsp (1,2 ml) hing
1 medium potato diced into about 1 cm cubes
1 medium carrot diced into small 1 cm cubes
A few green beans (approx 50 g) cut into
small rounds
¼ cup (60 ml) freshly boiled or frozen corn kernels
2 cups (500 ml) basmati rice
4 cups (1000 ml) boiling water
1 tsp (5 ml) salt
¼ cup (60 ml) freshly boiled or frozen green peas
1 tbs (15 ml) finely chopped fresh coriander

- Heat the oil or ghee in a medium-sized saucepan. Add the cumin seeds followed by the cinnamon stick, cardamom, black pepper, turmeric powder and hing.
- Add the vegetables (except the green peas) and rice. Braise for a few moments.
- Add the boiling water and salt.
- Stir once, add the green peas, cover and gently simmer over a very low heat for about 12 minutes until all the water is absorbed and the rice grains are fluffy and white.
- Gently toss with a fork and garnish with coriander.

Serving suggestion: Serve as a meal on its own, accompanied with green salad and nut, tamarind and fresh mint chutney.

Vegetable Rice (Biryani)

Here is a traditional biryani recipe. The cooking procedure takes place in three steps, precooking the rice, frying the vegetables and lastly, preparing the spices and assembling. The biryani is cooked in three layers and folded together before serving.

Preparation time : 45 minutes
Serves : 4 - 6 persons

Step One: Precooking the rice

3 cups (750 ml) water
I tsp (5 ml) salt
½ tsp (2,5 ml) hing
4 cloves
4 opened cardamom pods
I cinamon stick (3 inches)
I tsp (5 ml) oil or ghee
2 cups (500 ml) basmati rice

- Bring the water, salt, hing, cloves, cardamom, cinamon stick and oil or ghee to a gentle boil.
- Stir in the rice, cover and simmer over a low heat for about 12 minutes until all the water is absorbed and the rice grains are fluffy and white.
- Gently toss with a fork.

Step Two: Preparing the vegetables

4 medium potatoes (approx 460 g) peeled and diced into about 2 cm cubes
I cup (250 ml) or approx 115 g green beans cut into long thin strips
I cup (250 ml) or approx 115 g carrots cut into long thin strips
I cup (250 ml) soya chunks

- Lightly salt the potatoes and deep-fry until soft and golden brown.
- Lightly salt the carrots and green beans. Deep-fry until soft yet crisp.
- Boil the soya chunks until soft. Drain and squeeze out the excess water. Cut into smaller pieces, lightly salt and deep-fry until golden brown and crisp.

Step three: Preparing the spices and assembling

I ¼ cup (310 ml) water
¼ cup (60 ml) cumin seeds
I small piece fresh ginger (approx 2 cm)
2 tbs (30 ml) oil or ghee
I chili sliced into half
½ tsp (2,5 ml) hing
½ tsp (2,5 ml) salt
¼ tsp (1,2 ml) yellow food colour
½ cup (approx 125 ml) loosely packed fresh coriander finely chopped
½ cup (approx 125 ml) loosely packed fresh mint finely chopped

- Add a ¼ cup (60 ml) of the water to the cumin seeds and ginger, then grind into a fine paste.
- Heat the oil or ghee in a large heavy-based saucepan.
- Add the chili followed by the cumin and ginger paste, hing and salt.
- Fry for a few minutes, then add the vegetables, soya and remaining water.
- Add the rice layer, food colour, coriander and mint.
- Cover and simmer for about 10 minutes over a low heat or until the water has dried up.
- Before serving, gently fold the vegetables and soya with the rice.

Rice & Dhal Stew (Khichari)
A complete meal all in one made with dhal and vegetables.

Preparation time : 30 minutes
Serves : 4 - 6 persons

Step One
1 cup (250 ml) dhal soaked overnight, then drained
1 cup (250 ml) basmati rice
2 medium carrots diced into small cubes
A few green beans (approx 50 g) cut into
diagonal slices
1 small bunch of spinach (approx 50 g) finely chopped
1 medium potato peeled and diced into small cubes
4 cups (1000 ml) water
2 tsp (10 ml) salt
1 tsp (5 ml) oil or ghee

• Pressure-cook all the ingredients
  for 10 -15 minutes.

Step Two
2 tbs (15 ml) oil or ghee
½ tsp (2,5 ml) mustard seeds
1 tsp (5 ml) cumin seeds

1 chili finely chopped
1 medium tomato finely diced
½ tsp (2,5 ml) hing
1 tsp (5 ml) turmeric powder
1 tsp (5 ml) coriander powder
1 tbs (15 ml) finely chopped fresh coriander

• Heat the oil or ghee in a medium-sized saucepan.
• Add the mustard seeds and when they begin to
  splutter, add the cumin seeds followed by the chili.
• Add the tomato and sauté until soft and velvety.
• Add the hing, turmeric powder and coriander
  powder.
• Fold in the rice and dhal. Simmer for 5 minutes.
• Garnish with coriander.

Serving suggestion : Serve with chutney, pickles,
yoghurt and papadams.

Tomato Rice with Fresh Thyme
A tasty rice dish with tomato and fresh herbs.

Preparation time : 20 minutes
Serves : 4 - 6 persons

2 tbs (30 ml) olive oil
3 sprigs fresh thyme
¼ tsp (1,2 ml) black pepper
¼ tsp (1,2 ml) hing
2 medium tomatoes finely diced
2 tbs (30 ml) tomato purée
4 cups (1000 ml) water
1 tsp (5 ml) salt
2 cups (500 ml) basmati rice
¼ cup (60 ml) freshly boiled or frozen corn kernels
(optional)
¼ cup (60 ml) freshly boiled or frozen green peas
(optional)

• Heat the olive oil in a medium-sized saucepan.
• Add the thyme, black pepper and hing followed
  by the tomato and tomato purée. Sauté until soft
  and velvety.
• Add the water and salt. Bring to a gentle boil.
• Stir in the rice, corn and peas.
• Cover and simmer over a low heat for about
  12 minutes until all the water is absorbed and
  the rice grains are fluffy and white.
• Gently toss with a fork.

A non-grain preparation that can be used as a substitute for rice.
The soaked sago resembles grains of rice when mixed with vegetables.

Preparation time : 30 minutes
Soaking time : 1 hour
Serves : 4 - 6 persons

2 cups (500 ml) sago
2 medium carrots (approx 100 g) cut into long
thin strips.
1 medium eggplant (approx 120 g) diced into about
1 ½ cm cubes and lightly salted
1 small cauliflower (approx 115 g) cut into
small florets.
2 medium potatoes (approx 230 g) peeled and cut
into thin chips
¼ cup (60 ml) raw nuts lightly salted
1 tbs (15 ml) oil or ghee
6 - 8 curry leaves
1 chili finely chopped
1 sprig of fresh thyme
1 cup (250 ml) finely shredded cabbage
1 medium tomato finely diced
1 tsp (5 ml) salt
1 tbs (15 ml) finely chopped fresh coriander

• Soak the sago in water for at least one hour,
  then drain in a colander.
• Deep-fry the carrots, eggplant, cauliflower,
  potatoes and nuts. Drain and set aside.
• Heat oil or ghee in medium-sized heavy-based
  saucepan.
• Add curry leaves, chili and thyme followed
  by the cabbage and tomato. Sauté until soft.
• Mix in the deep-fry vegetables and nuts,
  then turn off the heat.
• Fold in the sago and salt.
• Garnish with coriander.

Serving suggestion : Serve with peanut chutney
and potato patties.

Cabbage Balls in Tomato Sauce (Cabbage Kofta)

Vegetable dishes

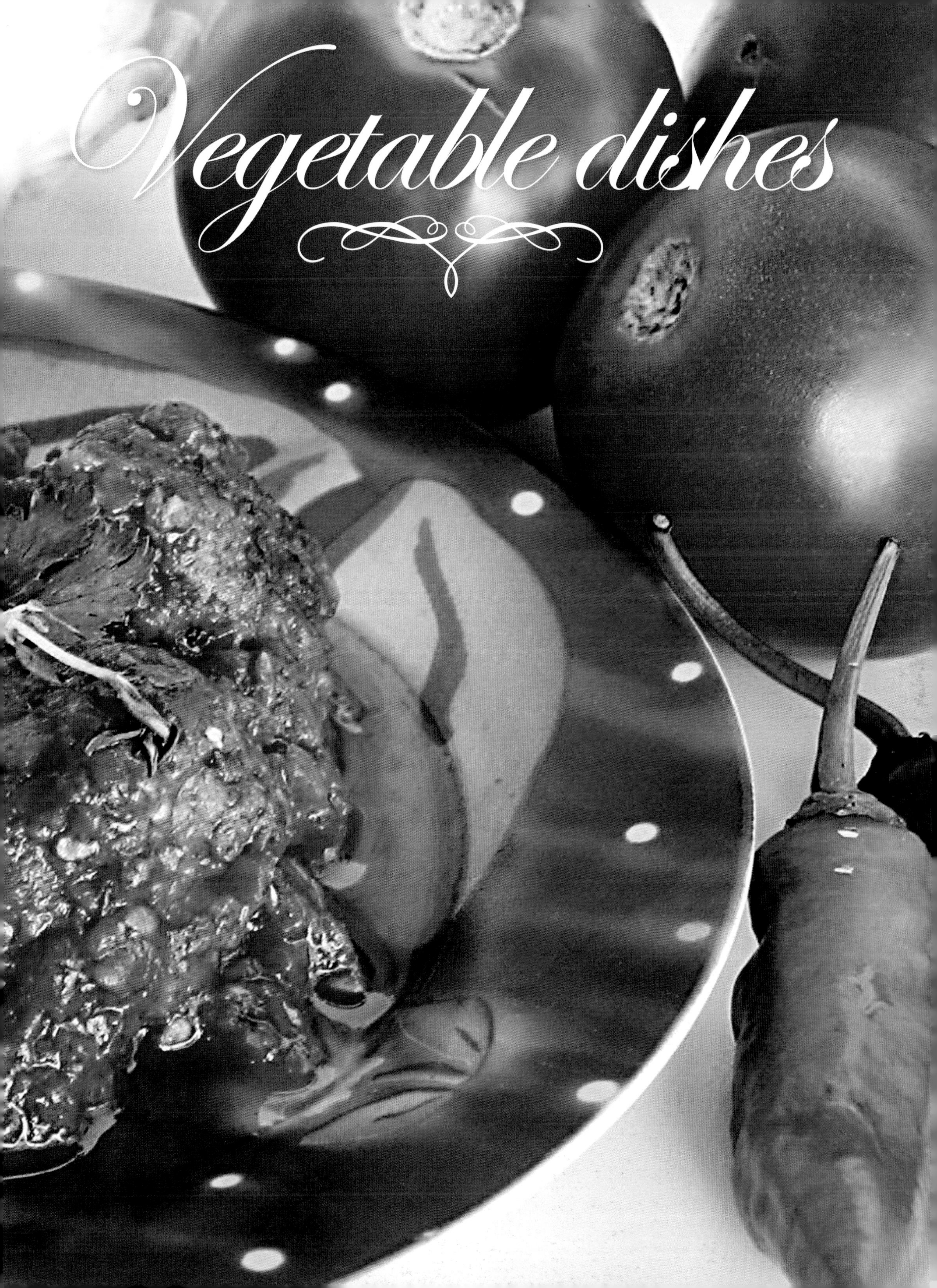

Red Kidney Beans and Eggplant Stew

Although red kidney beans are sold commercially ready cooked in a can, preparing the beans yourself adds a greater dimension to the taste. Soaking the beans overnight will lessen the cooking time and is more economical.

Preparation time : 30 minutes
Soaking time : overnight
Serves : 4 - 6 persons

Step One

1 cup (250 ml) red kidney beans soaked overnight, then drained
2 medium potatoes peeled and diced into about 1 ½ cm cubes
1 medium eggplant (approx 100g) cut into long strips
2 cups (500 ml) water
1 ½ tsp (7,5 ml) salt
1 tsp (5 ml) oil or ghee

• Pressure-cook all the ingredients together for 15 - 20 minutes.

Step Two

1 tbs (15 ml) oil or ghee
¼ tsp (1,2 ml) mustard seeds
¼ tsp (1,2 ml) cumin seeds
¼ tsp (1,2 ml) ajwain seeds
1 chili finely chopped
4 - 6 curry leaves
1 tsp (5 ml) turmeric powder
¼ tsp (1,2 ml) hing
1 medium tomato finely diced
1 tbs (15 ml) finely chopped fresh coriander

• Heat the oil or ghee in a medium-sized heavy-based saucepan.
• Add the mustard seeds and when they begin to splutter, add the cumin seeds and ajwain seeds followed by the chili and curry leaves.
• Add the turmeric powder, hing and tomato. Sauté until soft and velvety.

• Fold the beans in the mixture and simmer for 2 minutes so that the flavours can be absorbed.
• Garnish with coriander.

Serving suggestions : Serve as a protein dish to accompany rice and other vegetable preparations.

* Variations: Use other beans such as white kidney beans.

Alternative methods of cooking:

1. For unsoaked beans, pressure-cook the beans for at least 15 minutes before adding the vegetables. Then pressure-cook for a further 15 minutes.

2. If you are not using a pressure-cooker double the water and allow the beans to gently boil with the lid on for at least an hour for unsoaked beans or 30 minutes for soaked beans. Add the vegetables when the beans are three-quarter cooked.

3. If you prefer to use canned beans, add the vegetables first to the cooked spices with ½ cup (125 ml) water and gently cook until tender. Then fold in the beans and simmer for two more minutes.

White Kidney Beans and Potato Curry

A simple dish prepared with white broad kidney beans.

Preparation time : 30 minutes
Soaking time : overnight
Serves : 4 - 6 persons

*1 cup (250 ml) white kidney beans soaked overnight,
then drained*
*2 medium potatoes (230 g) peeled and diced into
about 1 ½ cm cubes*
2 cups (500 ml) water
1 tsp (5 ml) salt
4 tsp (20 ml) oil or ghee
1 chili finely chopped
6 - 8 curry leaves
¼ tsp (1,2 ml) hing
2 tbs (30 ml) curry powder or masala
1 tbs (15 ml) finely chopped fresh coriander

- Place the beans, potatoes, water and salt in
  a pressure-cooker along with 1 teaspoon (5 ml)
  of the oil or ghee and cook for 15 - 20 minutes.
- Heat the rest of the oil or ghee in a small
  saucepan. Add the chili and curry leaves followed
  by the hing and curry powder or masala.
- Fold the mixture into the bean stew and simmer
  for a few moments so that the flavours can
  be absorbed.
- Garnish with coriander.

Serving Suggestion : A wonderful curry to serve
with roti and cooked tomato chutney.

Bitter Melon and Potato Chips
with Freshly Ground Mustard

*Bitter melon, also known as Karela, is available in tropical countries. It is a rough green
knobbly vegetable that when ripe develops large red pips in the centre that should be removed
before cooking. As its name implies it is a very bitter vegetable and should be fried well before
serving. In India this vegetable is commonly taken to prevent diabetes.*

Preparation time : 30 minutes
Serves : 4 - 6 persons

*Approx 460 g bitter melon, seeded and cut into long,
thin strips*
*1 medium potato (approx 230 g) peeled and cut
into thin chips*
1 tsp (5 ml) salt
2 tbs (30 ml) oil or ghee
1 chili finely chopped
6 - 8 curry leaves
1 tbs (15 ml) freshly ground mustard seeds
½ tsp (2,5 ml) turmeric powder
¼ tsp (1,2 ml) hing
1 tbs (15 ml) finely chopped fresh coriander

- Sprinkle the bitter melon with ½ teaspoon
  (2,5 ml) of the salt and deep-fry until very crisp,
  then drain.

- Sprinkle the potato chips with remaining
  ½ teaspoon (2,5 ml) of the salt and deep-fry until
  golden brown, then drain.
- In a medium-sized heavy-based saucepan, heat
  the oil or ghee and fry the chili and curry leaves.
- Add the ground mustard seeds, turmeric powder
  and hing.
- Fold in the bitter melon and chips.
- Garnish with coriander.

Bitter Melon in Tomato Sauce
Deep-fried bitter melon goes well in a tomato sauce.

Approx 460 g bitter melon, seeded and cut into thin strips
1 tsp (5 ml) salt
2 tbs (30 ml) oil or ghee
¼ tsp (1,2 ml) mustard seeds
¼ tsp (1,2 ml) cumin seeds
1 chili finely chopped
6 - 8 curry leaves
¼ tsp (1,2 ml) hing
½ tsp (2,5 ml) turmeric powder
4 large tomatoes (460 g) blanched and puréed
1 tsp (5 ml) sugar
1 tbs (15 ml) finely chopped fresh coriander

• Sprinkle the bitter melon with ½ teaspoon (2,5 ml) of the salt and deep-fry until very crisp, then drain.
• Heat the oil or ghee in a medium-sized heavy-based saucepan.

• Add the mustard seeds and when they begin to splutter, add the cumin seeds followed by the chili and curry leaves.
• Add the hing, turmeric powder and tomato. Gently simmer for 10 minutes or until the tomato is well cooked.
• Fold in the bitter melon, sugar and remaining salt.
• Garnish with coriander.

Serving suggestion: Serve small amounts to accompany a meal as bitter melon is very pungent.

* *Variations: Add medium-sized cubes of deep-fried curd (115 g) made from 1 litre of full cream milk.*

Butternut and Cheese Balls
A light butternut dish with spicy curd balls.

Preparation time : 30 minutes
Serves : 4 - 6 persons

2 tbs (30 ml) oil or ghee
¼ tsp (1,2 ml) mustard seeds
¼ tsp (1,2 ml) cumin seeds
1 chili finely chopped
6 - 8 curry leaves
½ tsp (2,5 ml) finely grated ginger
¼ tsp (1,2 ml) hing
1 medium butternut (approx 690 g) peeled, seeded and diced into about 2 cm cubes
1 tsp (5 ml) salt
1 tbs (15 ml) finely chopped fresh coriander

• Heat the oil or ghee in a medium-sized heavy-based saucepan.
• Add the mustard seeds and when they begin to splutter, add the cumin seeds followed by the chili, curry leaves, ginger and hing.
• Fold in the butternut and salt.

• Simmer over low heat for about 20 minutes or until the butternut is soft.
• Add the cheese balls and garnish with coriander.

Preparing the cheese balls
115 g curd made from 1 litre full cream milk
1 tbs (15 ml) flour
¼ tsp (1,2 ml) hing
½ tsp (2,5 ml) ground cumin
½ tsp (2,5 ml) garam masala
¼ tsp (1,2 ml) salt
1 green chili finely chopped (optional)
1 tbs (15 ml) finely chopped fresh coriander

• Knead the curd until smooth.
• Mix in the rest of the ingredients and roll into small balls.
• Deep-fry in hot oil for a few seconds until golden brown, then drain.

*A special combination of spices and a generous amount
of ghee is required for this opulent dish.*

Preparation time : 30 minutes
Serves : 4 - 6 persons

*4 tbs (60 ml) ghee
1 small cabbage (approx 460 g) finely shredded
1 large potato (approx 175 g) peeled and diced
into about 1 ½ cm cubes
1 ½ tsp (7,5 ml) salt
1 tsp (5 ml) finely grated ginger
¼ tsp (1,2 ml) hing
1 medium tomato finely diced
1 tsp (5 ml) ground coriander
1 tsp (5 ml) ground cumin
1 tsp (5 ml) turmeric powder
½ cup (125 ml) water
1 tbs (15 ml) finely chopped fresh coriander*

- Heat 2 tablespoons (30 ml) of the ghee in
  a medium-sized saucepan. Add the cabbage,
  potatoes and salt. Braise for a few seconds.
- Cover and gently simmer over low heat,
  stirring occasionally until the vegetables are three
  quarter cooked.
- In a separate small saucepan, heat the remaining
  ghee. Add the ginger and hing followed by the
  tomato. Sauté until soft and velvety.
- Add the rest of the spices and water to form
  a paste.
- Fold the paste into the cabbage and potato
  preparation. Simmer for a further 5 minutes so
  that the flavours can be absorbed and until the
  potatoes are soft and well cooked.
- Garnish with coriander.

Serving suggestion: As this is rich curry the
accompaniments should be simple preparations
such as pumpkin and green peas or spinach
in white sauce.

** Variation: Add a handful of green peas towards
the end of the cooking.*

Cabbage Balls in Tomato Sauce (Cabbage Kofta)

Delicate balls of grated vegetable and chickpea flour, served in tomato sauce.

Preparation time : 30 minutes
Makes : 12 balls

2 cups (500 ml) finely grated cabbage
¾ cup (180 ml) chickpea flour
¼ tsp (1,2 ml) hing
1 tbs (15 ml) curry powder or masala
1 tbs (15 ml) finely chopped fresh coriander
¼ tsp (1,2 ml) bicarbonate of soda
1 tsp (5 ml) salt

• Squeeze out excess water from the grated cabbage.
• Mix in the remaining ingredients and form into 12 balls.
• Deep-fry over a medium heat until golden brown.
• Drain in a colander.

Preparing the tomato sauce

2 tbs (30 ml) oil or ghee
½ tsp (2,5 ml) mustard seeds
½ tsp (2,5 ml) cumin seeds
1 chili finely chopped
1 sprig fresh thyme
1 tsp (5 ml) finely grated ginger
1 tsp (5 ml) turmeric powder
¼ tsp (1,2 ml) hing
8 medium tomatoes (approx 920 g) blanched
and puréed
1 ½ tsp (7,5 ml) salt
2 tsp (10 ml) sugar
1 tbs (15 ml) finely chopped fresh coriander

• Heat the oil or ghee in a medium-sized saucepan.
• Add the mustard seeds and when they begin to splutter, add the cumin seeds, chili, thyme and ginger followed by the turmeric powder and hing.
• Add the tomato, salt and sugar. Allow to gently simmer for about 15 minutes or until the well cooked.
• Gently fold in the kofta balls and garnish with coriander.

Serving suggestion : Serve two kofta's per person.

* Variations : For the kofta balls, use different vegetables such as zucchini, calabash, chou chou or mixed vegetables instead of the cabbage.
Use 1 teaspoon (5 ml) of oregano and 1 tablespoon (15 ml) of freshly chopped parsley in place of curry powder or masala and coriander.
Replace the bicarbonate of soda by ½ teaspoon (2,5 ml) of baking powder.

Stuffed Cabbage Leaves

Quaint parcels of cabbage leaves with a homemade cheese filling, served in a tomato sauce.

Preparation time : 30 minutes
Serves : 4 - 6 persons

Preparing the stuffed cabbage leaves
6 large cabbage leaves
230 g curd made from 2 litres milk
2 tbs (30 ml) olive oil
¼ tsp (1,2 ml) black pepper
1 tsp (5 ml) salt
¼ tsp (1,2 ml) hing
1 tsp (5 ml) fresh thyme

- Remove the thick part of the stalk of each cabbage leaf.
- Blanch the leaves in lightly salted water, drain and allow to cool.
- Crumble the curd and fold in the rest of the ingredients.
- Spread the leaves out and place about 1 tablespoon (15 ml) of filling towards the bottom of each leaf. Fold the sides over and neatly roll up into parcels.
- Place in about a 5 cm deep serving dish.

Preparing the tomato sauce
1 tbs (15 ml) oil or ghee
¼ tsp (1,2 ml) mustard seeds
½ tsp (2,5 ml) cumin seeds
1 chili finely chopped
½ tsp (2,5 ml) freshly grated ginger
1 sprig of fresh thyme
¼ tsp (1,2 ml) hing
4 medium tomatoes (460 g) blanched and puréed
1 tsp (5 ml) salt
1 tsp (5 ml) sugar
1 tbs (15 ml) finely chopped parsley

- Heat the oil or ghee in a medium-sized heavy-based saucepan.
- Add the mustard seeds and when they begin to splutter, add the cumin seeds followed by the chili, ginger, thyme and hing.
- Fold in the tomato, salt and sugar. Simmer for about 10 minutes or until well cooked.
- Pour over the stuffed cabbage leaves.
- Garnish with parsley.

Serving suggestion : Excellent for a starter or serve as part of a main meal.

Bengali Style Cauliflower, Broccoli and Potato

The combination of freshly ground masala, butter and grated ginger is unique to this delicious curry.

Preparation time : 30 minutes
Serves : 4 - 6 persons

½ cup (125 ml) or100 g butter
1 tsp (5 ml) finely grated ginger
1 chili finely chopped (optional)
½ tsp (2,5 ml) hing
1 small cauliflower (approx 115 g) cut into
medium-sized florets
1 small broccoli (approx 115 g) cut into
medium-sized florets
2 medium potatoes (approx 230 g) peeled
and diced into about 2 cm cubes
1 tbs (15 ml) masala
1 tsp (5 ml) salt
1 tbs (15 ml) finely chopped fresh coriander

• Melt butter in a heavy-based saucepan and turn
  down the heat to low.
• Add the ginger, chili and hing followed by cauliflower,
  broccoli and potatoes. Braise for a few seconds.
• Fold in the masala and salt.
• Simmer over low heat with the lid on until the
  vegetables are tender yet crisp. Occasionally stir
  to prevent scorching.
• Garnish with coriander.

Preparing the masala
2 tbs (30 ml) cumin seeds
2 tbs (30 ml) coriander seeds
1 tbs (15 ml) fenugreek seeds
1 tbs (15 ml) fennel seeds
½ tbs (7,5 ml) opened cardamom pods
½ tbs (7,5 ml) cloves
½ tbs (7,5 ml) grated nutmeg
1 small cinnamon stick (approx 5 cm)
3 tbs (45 ml) turmeric powder

• Grind all the spices into a fine powder.
  This recipe makes 3 tablespoons (45 ml)
  and should be stored in an airtight container.

Serving suggestion : Serve with fancy rice, dhal
and wholewheat pooris.

Cauliflower and Potato in Creamy White Sauce

The subtle flavours of fenugreek and turmeric in a velvety white sauce form the basis of this wonderful curry.

Preparation time : 30 minutes
Serves : 4 - 6 persons

1 medium cauliflower (approx 230 g) cut into medium-sized florets
2 medium potatoes (approx 230 g) peeled and diced into about 1 ½ cm cubes
2 tbs (30 ml) butter
½ tsp (2,5 ml) fenugreek seed
6 - 8 curry leaves
1 chili finely chopped
1 tsp (5 ml) turmeric powder
¼ tsp (1,2 ml) hing
2 tbs (30 ml) flour
2 cups (500 ml) cups milk
1 tsp (5 ml) salt
1 tbs (15 ml) finely chopped parsley

- Deep-fry the cauliflower and potatoes separately until soft and golden brown. Drain in a colander.

- Melt the butter in a heavy-based saucepan.
- Add the fenugreek seeds followed by the curry leaves and chili. Fry for a few seconds.
- Braise the turmeric powder, hing and flour in the butter and spices.
- Whisk in the milk and salt.
- Bring to boil and simmer, stirring occasionally until the sauce thickens.
- Fold in vegetables.
- Garnish with parsley.

Serving suggestion : Serve hot with wholewheat bread and fresh green salad.

* Variation : Steam the vegetables instead of frying them.

Cauliflower, Potato, Homemade Cheese and Cashews in Sour Cream

A luxurious dish for a special occasion.

Preparation time : 30 minutes
Serves : 4 - 6 persons

1 medium cauliflower (approx 345 g) cut in to medium-sized florets
2 medium potatoes (approx 230 g) peeled and diced into about 1 ½ cm cubes
2 tbs (30 ml) cashew nuts
115 g curd made from 1 litre full cream milk, diced into medium cubes
2 tbs (30 ml) oil or ghee
¼ tsp (1,2 ml) mustard seeds
½ tsp (2,5 ml) cumin seeds
¼ tsp (1,2 ml) fenugreek seeds
1 chili finely chopped
4 - 6 curry leaves
½ tsp (2,5 ml) finely grated ginger
½ tsp (2,5 ml) turmeric powder
¼ tsp (1,2 ml) hing

1 cup (250 ml) sour cream
½ tsp (2,5 ml) salt
1 tbs (15 ml) finely chopped fresh coriander

- Lightly salt and deep-fry the cauliflower, potatoes, cashew nuts and curd separately until golden brown, then drain in a colander.
- Heat the oil or ghee in a medium-sized heavy-based saucepan.
- Add the mustard seeds and when they begin to splutter, add the cumin seeds and fenugreek seeds followed by the chili, curry leaves and ginger.
- Add the turmeric powder and hing.
- Fold in the vegetables, nuts, sour cream, curd and salt. Gently simmer for 2 minutes.
- Garnish with coriander

Serving suggestion : Serve with sweet and sour vegetables, cabbage balls in tomato sauce and basmati rice.

VEGETABLE DISHES

Chickpeas with Homemade Cheese

Here is a simple way to turn ready cooked chickpeas into a delicious curry.

Preparation time : 25 minutes
Serves : 4 persons

2 tbs (30 ml) olive oil
¼ tsp (1,2 ml) cumin seeds
1 chili finely chopped (optional)
1 bay leaf
½ tsp (2,5 ml) turmeric powder
¼ tsp (1,2 ml) hing
1 medium tomato finely diced
1 can (430 g) ready cooked chickpeas
¼ cup (60 ml) water
1 tsp (5 ml) salt
115 g curd made from 1 litre full cream milk, diced into
medium- sized cubes and deep-fried until golden brown
1 tbs (15 ml) finely chopped fresh coriander

• Heat the olive oil in a medium-sized heavy-based
  saucepan and add the cumin seeds followed by
  the chili and bay leaf.

• Add the turmeric powder and hing.
• Add the tomato and sauté until soft and velvety.
• Fold in the chickpeas, water, salt and curd.
  Gently simmer for 15 minutes with the lid on.
• Garnish with coriander.

Serving suggestion : Serve on a bed of hot basmati rice.

Hint : Add ¼ teaspoon (1,2 ml) hing and ½ teaspoon
(5 ml) salt to the whey that is left from making the
curd. Add the deep-fried curd while hot to the warm
whey and allow to soak for about 10 - 15 minutes
or until they swell up and become more plump
and succulent.

Chickpeas, Tomato and Green Pepper Stew

Chickpeas are rich in protein and delicious when stewed with tomato and green peppers.

1 tbs (15 ml) oil or ghee
1 tsp (5 ml) mustard seeds
1 tsp (5 ml) cumin seeds
1 chili finely chopped
6 - 8 curry leaves
½ tsp (2,5 ml) finely grated ginger
½ tsp (2,5 ml) turmeric powder
¼ tsp (1,2 ml) hing
½ medium green pepper thinly sliced into long strips
4 medium tomatoes (approx 460 g) tomatoes
blanched and puréed
2 cups (500 ml) boiled chickpeas
1 ½ tsp (7,5 ml) salt
1 tsp (5 ml) sugar
1 tbs (15 ml) finely chopped fresh coriander or parsley

• Heat oil or ghee in a medium-sized heavy-based
  saucepan.
• Add mustard seeds and when they begin to
  splutter, add cumin seeds followed by the chili,
  curry leaves and ginger.
• Fry for a few moments, then add the turmeric
  powder and hing.
• Add the green peppers and sauté for a few
  moments more.
• Stir in the tomato purée and simmer for about
  5 minutes or until well cooked.
• Fold in the chickpeas, salt and sugar. Cook for
  a further 5 minutes so that the chickpeas can
  absorb the flavours of the tomato sauce.
• Garnish with coriander or parsley.

Stir-fried Chou Chou, Potato and Carrots

Chou chou belongs to the squash family and is widely available in tropical countries where it grows on creeper bushes. The vegetable has a spiky green skin that should be removed before cooking. Allow the chou chou to lie in water as you peel, as its residues can stain your hands.

Preparation time : 40 minutes
Serves : 4 - 6 persons

1 tbs (15 ml) oil or ghee
¼ tsp (1,2) mustard seeds
½ tsp (2,5 ml) cumin seeds
½ tsp (2,5 ml) fenugreek seeds
1 finely chopped chili (optional)
3 sprigs fresh thyme
¼ tsp (1,2 ml) hing

1 medium chou chou (approx 460 g) peeled and cut into very thin, broad and flat slices (approx 0,5 cm by 5 cm each)
2 medium potatoes (approx 230g) peeled and cut into very thin, broad and flat slices (approx 0,5 cm by 5 cm each)
2 medium carrots cut into thin broad slices

1 cup (250 ml) water
1 ½ tsp (7,5 ml) salt
1 tbs (15 ml) finely chopped fresh coriander

• Heat the oil or ghee in a medium-sized heavy-based saucepan.
• Add the mustard seeds and when they begin to splutter, add the cumin seeds and fenugreek seeds followed by chili, thyme and hing.
• Fold in the vegetables, water and salt. Simmer over a low heat with the lid on for about 20 minutes or until the vegetables are tender.
• Remove the lid and cook for another 10 minutes to evaporate any excess water.
• Garnish with coriander.

Cottage Pie

Lentil stew layered with mashed potato and topped with cheese, this dish makes a wonderful meal on its own.

Preparation time : 30 minutes
Baking time : 20 minutes
Serves : 4 - 6 persons

Step One: Preparing the lentil stew

1 tbs (15 ml) olive oil
1 bay leaf
¼ tsp (1,2 ml) hing
½ tsp (2,5 ml) turmeric powder
1 medium tomato finely diced
1 medium carrot cut into thin slices
1 can (410 g) ready cooked lentils
1 tsp (5 ml) salt

• Heat the olive oil in a medium-sized heavy-based saucepan.
• Add the bay leaf, hing and turmeric powder followed by the tomato and sauté until soft and velvety.
• Add the carrots, lentils and salt. Gently simmer for about 10 minutes.

Step Two: Preparing the mash potato

2 medium potatoes (approx 230 g) boiled, peeled and mashed
1 tbs (15 ml) milk
½ tsp (2,5 ml) salt
1 tbs (15 ml) butter

• Fold all the ingredients together.

Step Three: Assembling

• Place the lentil stew in a medium-sized dish (approx 12 cm by 18 cm).
• Spread the mash potato on top and sprinkle with ½ cup (125 ml) grated cheese.
• Place in a preheated moderate oven at 180° C or 350° F for about 20 minutes or until the cheese has melted and has speckles of golden brown.
• Garnish with parsley.

Dhal Croquettes in Curry Sauce (Curry Bari)
Spicy dhal balls are traditionally served with large eggplant strips in curry sauce.

Preparation time : 30 minutes
Soaking time : 3 hours
Makes : 15 balls

Step One : Preparing the balls
*1 cup (250 ml) yellow split pea dhal soaked for at least
3 hours, then drained*
¼ tsp (1,2 ml) hing
1 tbs (15 ml) finely chopped fresh coriander
6 - 8 curry leaves roughly chopped
1 chili finely chopped
¼ tsp (1,2 ml) bicarbonate of soda
1 tsp (5 ml) salt

• Blend the dhal into a smooth paste without
  adding any water. Keep aside about 2 tablespoons
  (30 ml) of the dhal paste for thickening the sauce.
• Mix all the ingredient together and roll into about
  15 balls.
• Deep-fry until crisp and golden brown, then drain.

Step Two : Preparing the sauce
2 tbs (30 ml) oil or ghee
½ tsp (2,5 ml) mustard seeds
1 chili finely chopped
½ tsp (2,5 ml) finely grated ginger
1 tsp (5 ml) fresh thyme
1 tbs (15 ml) turmeric powder
¼ tsp (1,2 ml) hing
1 medium tomato finely diced
2 tbs curry powder or masala
4 cups (1000 ml) water
1 ½ tsp (7,5 ml) salt
1 medium eggplant cut into long strips and deep-fry.
1 tbs (15 ml) finely chopped fresh coriander

• Heat the oil or ghee in a medium-sized saucepan.
• Add the mustard seeds and when they begin to
  splutter, add the chili, ginger, and thyme followed
  by the turmeric powder and hing.
• Add the tomato and sauté until soft and velvety
  followed by the curry powder or masala.
• Add the water, salt and dhal paste (as kept
  from above) and bring to a gentle boil for
  about 10 minutes, stirring occasionally until
  the sauce thickens.
• Add the eggplants and dhal balls.
• Garnish with coriander.

Serving suggestion : Serve as a protein dish with rice.

* Variations : Serve the dhal croquettes in tomato sauce.

Eggplant Parmesan
A layered eggplant dish that can be served as part of a meal.

Preparation time : 30 minutes
Baking time : 20 minutes
Serves : 4 - 6 persons

1 large eggplant (approx 230 g) sliced into thin rings
Pakora batter (see page 91)
Cooked tomato chutney (see page 85)
115 g grated curd made from 1 litre full cream milk
½ cup (125 ml) grated cheese
Parmesan cheese for sprinkling
1 tbs (15 ml) finely chopped parsely

• Coat each eggplant ring with pakora batter and
  deep-fry until golden brown and crisp, then drain.

• Layer a medium-sized dish (approx 12 cm
  by 18 cm) with alternative layers of eggplant
  pakoras, chutney and curd. There should be at least
  2 layers of each item.
• Sprinkle grated cheese and parmesan on top. Bake
  in a preheated moderate oven at 180° C or 350° F
  for about 20 minutes or until the cheese is melted
  and has speckles of golden brown.
• Garnish with parsley

Bengali Eggplant, Potato and Homemade Cheese in Cream Sauce

This curry features large chunks of deep-fried eggplant, potatoes and curd folded in fresh cream. A special spicing called 5 Spice (Panch Puran) is required. As with most deep-fried curries, sprinkling the salt on the vegetables before frying makes the dish tastier.

Preparation time : 30 minutes
Serves : 4 persons

*1 large eggplant (approx 230 g) diced into large
4 cm cubes
2 medium potatoes (approx 230 g) peeled and diced
into large 3 cm cubes
230 g of curd made from 2 litres milk, diced into large
3 cm cubes
1 tsp (5 ml) salt
1 tbs (15 ml) oil or ghee
1 tsp (5 ml) 5 spice (Panch Puran)
1 chili finely diced (optional)
½ tsp (2,5 ml) finely grated ginger
¼ tsp (1,2 ml) hing
1 tsp (5 ml) turmeric powder
1 cup (250 ml) fresh cream
1 tbs (15 ml) finely chopped fresh coriander*

- Sprinkle the eggplant and potatoes with half of the salt and allow to stand for 5 minutes.
- Deep-fry separately until tender, then drain.
- Sprinkle the curd with ¼ teaspoon (1,2 ml) of the salt. Deep-fry until golden brown. Soak in the whey for a few minutes to become more juicy and succulent.
- Heat the oil or ghee in a medium-sized saucepan. Add the 5 Spice and fry for a few moments.
- Add the chili and ginger followed by the hing and turmeric powder.
- Gently fold in the vegetables, curd, fresh cream and remaining ¼ teaspoon (1,2 ml) salt.
- Simmer for 2 minutes so that the flavours can be absorbed.
- Garnish with coriander.

5 Spice (Panch Puran)

A well proportioned combination of spices that is unique to Bengali cooking. This can be used to flavour other vegetable curries.

*3 tsp (15 ml) cumin seeds
3 tsp (15 ml) mustard seeds
3 tsp (15 ml) fennel seeds
1 tsp (5 ml) kalonji seeds
1 tsp (5 ml) fenugreek seeds*

- Mix all the spices together and keep in an airtight container until needed.

Serving suggestion : Serve with hot wholewheat pooris, basmati rice and dhal.

Eggplant with Chickpeas and Potato Filling, Served with Yoghurt Sauce

Here is a creative way to fill baked eggplants served with traditional yoghurt sauce, also known as kadhi sauce. This pleasant dish makes a wonderful East and West combination.

Preparation time : 30 minutes
Baking time : 45 minutes
Serves : 4 persons

2 large eggplants (approx 460 g)
3 ½ tsp (17,5 ml) salt
6 tbs (90 ml) olive oil
1 tsp (5 ml) fresh thyme
1 tsp (5 ml) finely grated ginger
1 medium tomato finely diced
2 medium potatoes (approx 230 g) boiled, peeled and mashed
1 cup (250 ml) cooked chickpeas

- Halve the eggplants and scoop out the centres, leaving the cases. Retain the scooped-out parts for the filling.
- Sprinkle the eggplant cases with 2 teaspoons (10 ml) of the salt. Allow to stand for about 10 minutes, then rinse.
- Place on a baking tray and liberally baste with 4 tablespoons (60 ml) of the olive oil.
- Bake in a moderate oven at 180° C or 350° F for about 45 minutes or until tender.
- Heat the remaining olive oil in a medium-sized heavy-based saucepan.
- Add the thyme and ginger followed by the scooped-out parts of the eggplants and tomato. Sauté until soft and velvety.
- Fold in potatoes, chickpeas and remaining salt.
- Fill each eggplant case with a generous helping of filling.

For the yoghurt sauce

1 tbs (15 ml) oil or ghee
¼ tsp (1,2 ml) mustard seeds
1 chili finely chopped
4 - 6 curry leaves
½ tsp (2,5 ml) turmeric powder
¼ tsp (1,2 ml) hing
1 cup (250 ml) yoghurt
1 tsp (5 ml) sugar
1 tsp (5 ml) salt
Approx ½ cup (125 ml) water
1 tbs (15 ml) finely chopped parsley

- Heat the oil or ghee in a small heavy-based saucepan.
- Add the mustard seeds and when they begin to splutter, add the chili and curry leaves followed by the turmeric powder and hing.
- Fold in the yoghurt, sugar, salt and enough water to make a thick sauce. Gently simmer for 2 minutes so that the flavours can be absorbed.
- Pour the sauce over the eggplant preparation and garnish with parsley.

Serving suggestion : Serve with fresh green salad.

Gauranga Ananda Swoon

The name means to faint in the bliss of Gauranga (love of God through chanting His Holy Name).

Preparation time : 20 minutes
Baking time : 55 minutes
Serves : 4 persons

Step One

2 large eggplants (approx 200 g each)
2 tbs (30 ml) olive oil
½ tsp (2,5 ml) salt

- Cut the eggplants in half. Scoop out the insides. Retain the scooped-out part for the filling.
- Sprinkle the cases with salt. Leave for 10 minutes, then rinse.
- Place the cases on a baking tray and baste with olive oil.
- Bake in a preheated moderate oven at 180° C or 350° F for about 45 minutes or until tender.

Step Two

3 tbs (45 ml) olive oil
1 medium tomato finely diced
2 cups (500 ml) bread crumbs
2 tbs (30 ml) pine nuts lightly roasted
½ tsp (2,5 ml) salt
¼ tsp (1,2 ml) black pepper
Parmesan cheese for sprinkling
1 tbs (15 ml) finely chopped parsley

- Heat the olive oil in a medium-sized heavy-based saucepan.
- Add the scooped-out eggplant filling and tomato. Sauté until soft.
- Fold in the bread crumbs, pine nuts, salt and black pepper.
- Fill the eggplant cases with a generous amount of filling.
- Sprinkle with parmesan cheese. Bake for a further 10 minutes or until golden brown.
- Garnish with parsley.

Serving suggestion : Serve as a starter or as a main course at a special dinner.

* *Variations : Use chickpeas in place of bread crumbs. Omit the pine nuts.*

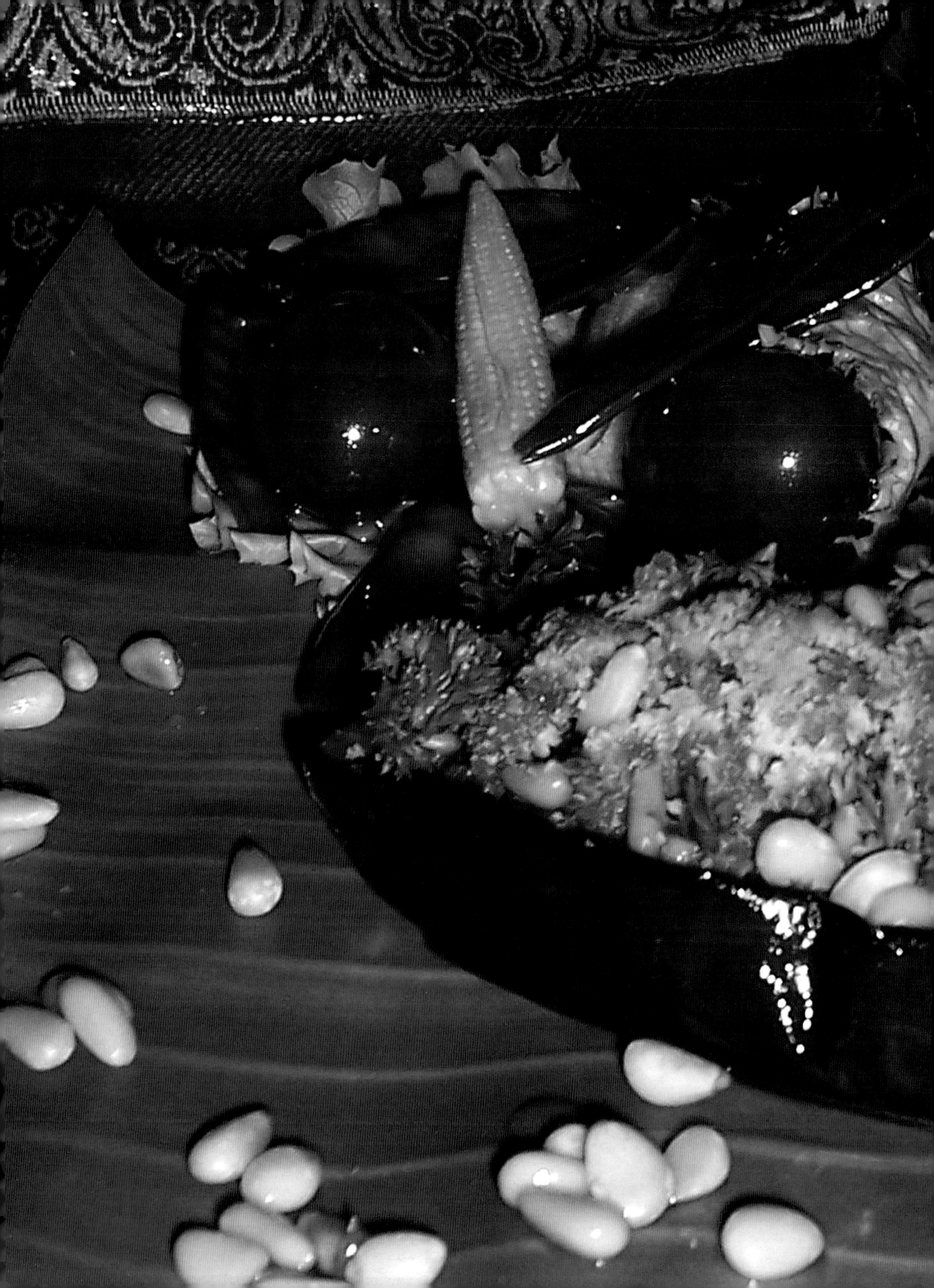

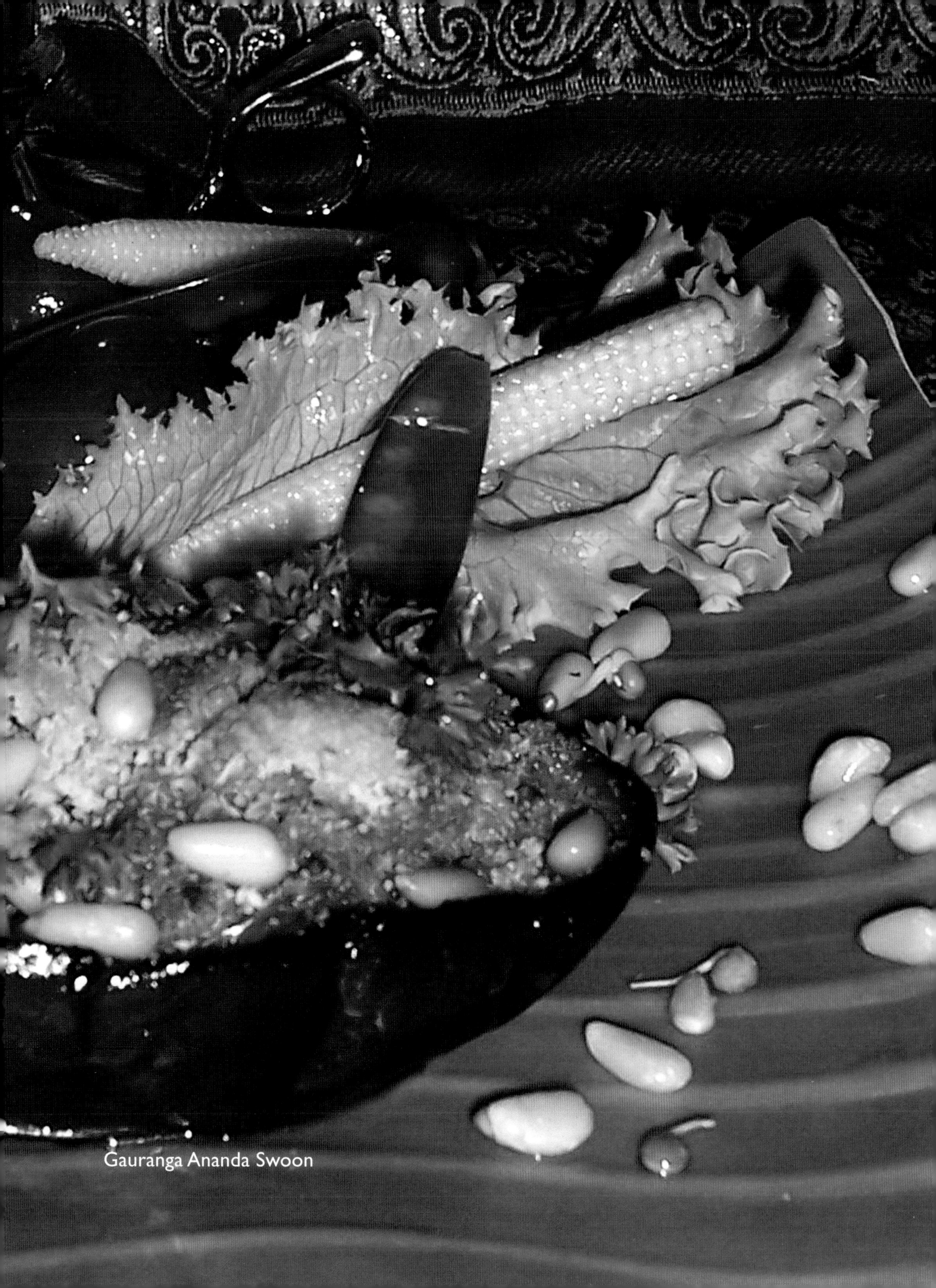

Gauranga Ananda Swoon

Patta Leaf Curry

Patta leaves are also known as khachoo or madumbi leaves. They are similar to spinach but grow on marshy lands. A good amount of tomato and tamarind should be used to neutralise its scratchiness. Large spinach leaves can be used to substitute the patta leaves.

Preparation time : 45 minutes
Serves : 4 - 6 persons

1 large bunch (approx 460 g) patta leaves
2 ¼ cup (560 ml) water
1 tbs (15 ml) oil or ghee
¼ tsp (1,2 ml) fenugreek seeds
1 chili finely chopped
4 - 6 curry leaves
1 tsp (5 ml) ginger finely grated
¼ tsp (1,2 ml) hing
2 medium tomatoes (approx 230 g) pureed
1 tsp (5 ml) salt
1 tbs (15 ml) tamarind

- Separate the patta leaves from their stems. Chop and wash the leaves.
- Pressure-cook in 2 cups (500 ml) of the water for about 10 - 15 minutes, then drain.

- Heat oil or ghee in a medium-sized heavy-based saucepan.
- Fry the fenugreek seeds followed by the chili, curry leaves, ginger and hing.
- Add the tomato and sauté until well cooked.
- Fold in the leaves and salt. Cook for a further 15 minutes or until velvety.
- Soak the tamarind in the remaining ¼ cup (60 ml) water and strain from pips.
- Add the tamarind water to the patta curry and simmer a further 5 minutes.

Serving suggestion: Serve with Indian bread or basmati rice.

An irresistible curry made by folding homemade cheese into a rich cream sauce. The curd can be used unfried but fried curd will make a richer and tastier curry.

Preparation time : 30 minutes
Serves : 4 - 6 persons

230 g curd made from 2 litres full cream milk, diced into medium cubes
¼ cup (60 ml) or 50 g butter
1 chili finely chopped (optional)
6 - 8 curry leaves
1 tsp (5 ml) turmeric powder
¼ tsp (1,2 ml) hing
2 medium tomatoes (approx 230 g) puréed
2 cups (500 ml) fresh cream
1 tsp (5 ml) salt
¼ tsp (1,2 ml) fenugreek powder (optional)
1 tbs (15 ml) finely chopped fresh coriander

- Deep-fry the curd until golden brown, then drain and soak in lightly salted warm whey until plump.

- Melt the butter in a medium-sized heavy-based saucepan.
- Add the chili, curry leaves, turmeric powder and hing followed by the tomato. Sauté for 2 minutes or until well cooked.
- Fold in the cream, salt and soaked curd. Allow to simmer for another 2 minutes.
- Turn off the heat and fold in the fenugreek powder.
- Garnish with coriander.

Serving suggestion: Serve with saffron, pea and cashew rice and vegetarian 'fish' curry.

Homemade Cheese, Green Peas and Tomato Stew (Matar Panir)

Curd, green peas and tomato curry is an opulent dish.

Preparation time : 30 minutes
Serves : 4 - 6 persons

2 tbs (30 ml) oil or ghee
1 tsp (5 ml) mustard seeds
1 tsp (5 ml) cumin seeds
1 chili finely chopped
½ tsp (2,5 ml) finely grated ginger
1 sprig fresh thyme
1 tsp (5 ml) turmeric powder
¼ tsp (1,2 ml) hing
8 medium tomatoes (approx 920 g) blanched
and puréed
1 tsp (5 ml) sugar
1 tsp (5 ml) salt
230 g curd made from 2 litres full cream milk,
diced into medium cubes
1 ½ cup (375 ml) freshly boiled or frozen green peas
1 tbs (15 ml) roughly chopped fresh mint

- Heat the oil or ghee in a medium-sized heavy-based saucepan.
- Add the mustard seeds and when they begin to splutter, add the cumin seeds followed by the chili, ginger and thyme.
- Add the turmeric powder and hing.
- Fold in the tomato, sugar and salt. Simmer for about 15 minutes or until well cooked.
- Deep-fry the curd until golden brown, then drain and soak in lightly salted warm whey until plump.
- Fold the curd and green peas into the tomato. Simmer for a further 5 minutes.
- Garnish with mint.

Jackfruit and Potato Curry

Jackfriut is available in tropical countries where it can grow very large weighing up to 5 kg or more.

Preparation time : 30 minutes
Serves : 6 - 8 persons

2 tbs (30 ml) oil or ghee
½ tsp (2,5 ml) mustard seeds
½ tsp (2,5 ml) fenugreek seeds
1 chili finely chopped
6 - 8 curry leaves
1 tsp (5 ml) finely grated ginger
1 ½ tbs (22,5 ml) cumin seeds ground into a fine powder
2 tsp (10 ml) turmeric powder
½ tsp (2,5 ml) hing
2 tbs (30 ml) curry powder or masala
1 small jackfruit (approx 460 g) peeled, cord and cut into 2 cm segments
2 medium potatoes (approx 230 g) peeled and diced into about 2 cm cubes
2 cups (500 ml) water
2 tsp (10 ml) salt
2 medium tomatoes (approx 230 g) finely diced
1 tbs (15 ml) finely chopped fresh coriander

• Heat oil or ghee in a large heavy-based saucepan.
• Add the mustard seed and when they begin to splutter, add the fenugreek seeds followed by the chili, curry leaves and ginger. Fry for a few moments.
• Add the cumin powder, turmeric powder, hing and curry powder or masala.
• Fold in the jackfruit and potatoes.
• Add the water and salt, then bring to boil.
• Reduce the heat and simmer with the lid on for about 15 - 20 minutes or until the vegetables are soft. Occasionally give a stir to allow even cooking.
• Add the tomato three quarter way through the cooking.
• Garnish with coriander.

Hint: The cooking time depends on the tenderness of the jackfruit. More water can be added if the curry is taking longer to cook.

Jackfruit and Potato Curry

Green Bananas and Potato Chips with Freshly Ground Mustard

Green banana can be prepared into a delicious curry. This recipe calls for blanching and grating the bananas, then adding pickle spices for its seasoning.

Preparation time : 30 minutes
Serves : 4 - 6 persons

6 large green bananas (approx 690 g)
2 medium potatoes (approx 230 g) peeled and cut into about 1 cm by 5 cm chips
2 tbs (30 ml) oil or ghee
1 chili finely chopped
6 - 8 curry leaves
2 tbs (30 ml) freshly ground mustard seeds
¼ tsp (1,2 ml) hing
1 ½ tsp (7,5 ml) turmeric powder
1 tsp (5 ml) salt
1 tbs (15 ml) finely chopped fresh coriander

- Cut off the ends of the bananas. Make a slit in the skin down the side of each banana.

- Gently boil for about 10 minutes or until the inside of the bananas are cooked but still firm. Drain and cool. Remove the peels and grate coarsely.
- Deep-fry the potatoes until golden brown, then drain.
- Heat the oil or ghee in a medium-sized heavy-based saucepan.
- Add the chili and curry leaves followed by the ground mustard, hing and turmeric powder.
- Fold in the vegetables and salt.
- Garnish with coriander.

Green Bananas and Potato Chips with Freshly Ground Mustard

Okra, Potato and Carrots

Okra, a green pod-like vegetable, is the prominent vegetable of this dish.
Always choose tender ones for cooking.

Preparation time : 30 minutes
Serves : 4 - 6 persons

2 tbs (30 ml) oil or ghee
¼ tsp (1,2 ml) mustard seeds
½ tsp (2,5 ml) cumin seeds
¼ tsp (1,2 ml) fenugreek seeds
1 chili finely chopped
4 - 6 curry leaves
1 tsp (5 ml) turmeric powder
¼ tsp (1,2 ml) hing

Approx 460 g okra washed and patted dried with
a cloth, then cut into about 2 cm segments. Sprinkle
with ½ tsp (2,5 ml) salt, deep-fry until tender yet crisp,
then drain.

3 medium carrots (approx 100 g) diced into about
1 ½ cm cubes. Sprinkle with ½ tsp (2,5 ml) salt
and deep-fry as above.

1 medium potato (approx 115 g) peeled and diced
into about 1 ½ cm cubes. Sprinkle with ½ tsp (2,5 ml)
salt and deep-fry as above.

1 tbs (15 ml) finely chopped fresh coriander

- Heat the oil or ghee in a medium-sized saucepan.
- Add the mustard seeds and when they begin to
  splutter, add the cumin seeds and fenugreek seeds
  followed by the chili and curry leaves.
- Add the turmeric powder and hing.
- Fold in the fried vegetables.
- Garnish with coriander.

* *Variations: Deep-fry a ¼ cup (60 ml) of lightly salted*
  raw nuts and add to the curry.

Stuffed Patole

Almost any vegetable can be stuffed by scooping out its insides and deep-frying
or baking the shells. Here is a recipe with patole and spicy homemade cheese filling.

Preparation time : 30 minutes
Makes : 10 pieces
2 medium patole (approx 460 g) scraped and cut
into 5 cm rounds
2 tbs (30 ml) oil or ghee
½ tsp (2,5 ml) mustard seeds
1 chili finely chopped
6 - 8 curry leaves
1 tsp (5 ml) turmeric powder
½ tsp (2,5 ml) hing
230 g curd made from 2 litres milk, then crumbled
1 tsp (5 ml) salt
1 tbs (15 ml) finely chopped fresh coriander

- Scoop out the inside of the patole.
- Lightly salt the patole and deep-fry until tender,
  then drain.
- Heat the oil or ghee in a medium-sized heavy-

based saucepan.
- Add the mustard seeds and when they begin
  to splutter, add the chili and curry leaves followed
  by the turmeric powder and hing.
- Fold in the curd, salt and coriander.
- Fill the patole with a generous amount of curd
  mixture.

Serving suggestion: Place in an attractive dish and
pour over tomato sauce (see page 48). Garnish with
fresh coriander.

Potato Stir-fry

Potato chips can be made into a stir-fried curry that can be served with freshly baked bread.

Preparation time : 30 minutes
Serves : 4 persons

2 tbs (30 ml) oil or ghee
¼ tsp (1,2 ml) mustard seeds
½ tsp (2,5 ml) cumin seeds
I chili finely chopped (optional)
4 - 6 curry leaves
½ tsp (2,5 ml) finely grated ginger
¼ tsp (1,2 ml) hing
4 medium potatoes (approx 460 g) peeled and cut into flat and thin chips
I ½ tsp (7,5 ml) salt
I tbs (15 ml) finely chopped fresh coriander

- Heat the oil or ghee in a medium-sized wok.
- Add the mustard seeds and when they begin to splutter, add the cumin seeds followed by the chili, curry leaves, ginger and hing.
- Fold in the potato chips and salt.
- Cover and allow to cook over a gentle heat for about 15 minutes or until the potatoes are well cooked. Toss occasionally to prevent scorching.
- Garnish with coriander.

Pumpkin with Green Peas

Simple pumpkin curry cooked down to a velvety texture. Try this version with green peas and a sprig of thyme.

Preparation time : 20 minutes
Serves : 4 - 6 persons

I tbs (15 ml) oil or ghee
¼ tsp (1,2 ml) mustard seeds
½ tsp (2,5 ml) cumin seeds
¼ tsp (1,2 ml) fenugreek seeds
I chili finely chopped
6 - 8 curry leaves
½ tsp (2,5 ml) finely grated ginger
I sprig of fresh thyme
Approx 920 g pumpkin peeled, seeded and diced into about 2 cm cubes
½ tsp (2,5 ml) salt
½ cup (125 ml) freshly boiled or frozen green peas
½ tbs (7,5 ml) finely chopped fresh coriander

- Heat oil or ghee in a medium-sized heavy-based saucepan.
- Add mustard seeds and when they begin to splutter, add the cumin seeds and fenugreek seeds followed by the chili, curry leaves, ginger and thyme.
- Fold in the pumpkin and salt.
- Turn down the heat, cover and simmer for about 15 minutes, stirring occasionally or until the pumpkin is cooked down to a velvety texture.
- Gently fold in the green peas and cook for a few more moments before turning off the heat.
- Garnish with coriander.

* *Variation: Replace the green peas with ½ cup (125 ml) of boiled chickpeas.*

VEGETABLE DISHES

Soya, Green Peas and Tomato Stew
Use dehydrated soya chunks available at most health stores.

Preparation time : 30 minutes
Serves : 4 persons

1 cup (250 ml) soya chunks
1 ½ tsp (7,5 ml) salt
2 tbs (30 ml) oil or ghee
¼ tsp (1,2 ml) mustard seeds
½ tsp (2,5 ml) cumin seeds
1 chili finely chopped
4 - 6 curry leaves
½ tsp (2,5 ml) finely grated ginger
¼ tsp (1,2 ml) hing
½ tsp (2,5 ml) turmeric powder
2 medium tomatoes (approx 230 g) finely diced
½ cup (125 ml) freshly boiled or frozen green peas
1 tbs (15 ml) finely chopped fresh coriander

- Boil the soya chunks until soft. Drain and squeeze out the excess water.
- Sprinkle with 1 teaspoon (5 ml) of the salt and deep-fry until golden brown and crisp.
- Heat the oil or ghee in a medium-sized heavy-based saucepan.
- Add the mustard seeds and when they begin to splutter, add the cumin seeds, chili, curry leaves, and ginger followed by the hing and turmeric powder.
- Add the tomato and sauté until soft and velvety.
- Fold in the soya, green peas and remaining salt.
- Garnish with coriander.

Spinach and Cheese Balls (Malai Kofta)
This dish is ideal for large gatherings.

Preparation time : 30 minutes
Makes : 18 balls

For the Kofta Balls
2 large bunches of spinach (approx 230 g) finely chopped
230 g curd made from 2 litres milk
1 chili finely chopped
1 tsp (5 ml) finely grated ginger
1 tsp (5 ml) garam masala
¼ tsp (1,2 ml) hing
1 ½ tsp (7,5 ml) salt
¼ cup (60 ml) chickpea flour

- Steam the spinach and drain.
- Crumble the curd and add the spinach, chili, ginger, masala, hing and salt.

- Place in a food processor and pulsate in two short bursts so that the mixture becomes more compressed but the spinach is still whole. Alternatively, knead the mixture with your hands until the curd and spinach can hold together.
- Mix in the chickpea flour and roll into approx 18 balls.
- Deep-fry in moderate hot oil until golden brown. Handle the balls gently in the oil and fry small batches at a time, then drain.

Serving suggestions : Gently fold the kofta in tomato sauce (see page 48) and garnish with fresh coriander.

Spinach in Cream Sauce (Palak Panir)

The irresistible flavour when combining fresh cream with butter, turmeric and tomato forms the bases of this luxurious curry.

Preparation time : 30 minutes
Serves : 4 persons

2 large bunches spinach (approx 230 g)
1 tbs (30 ml) butter
1 chili finely chopped (optional)
½ tsp (2,5 ml) finely grated ginger (optional)
1 medium tomato finely diced
1 tsp (5 ml) turmeric powder
¼ tsp (1,2 ml) hing
1 cup (250 ml) fresh cream
1 ½ tsp (7,5 ml) salt
115 g curd made from 1 litre milk, diced into medium cubes
¼ tsp (2,5 ml) fenugreek powder (optional)

- Steam the spinach, drain and purée.
- Heat the butter in a medium-sized heavy-based saucepan.
- Add the chili, ginger, tomato, turmeric powder and hing. Sauté until the tomato is soft and velvety.
- Fold in the cream and salt. Bring to a gentle boil.
- Fold in the spinach and the curd. Simmer for a few moments.
- Add the fenugreek powder at the end of the cooking.

Serving suggestion: Serve as part of a special Eastern meal.

Spinach and Potato with Fresh Ginger

This is a simple spinach dish.

Preparation time : 30 minutes
Serves : 2 - 4 persons

1 tbs (15 ml) oil or ghee
1 chili finely chopped
½ tsp (2,5 ml) finely grated ginger or cut into small squares
¼ tsp (1,2 ml) hing
1 medium potato peeled and cut into chips
2 bunches spinach (approx 230 g) roughly chopped
1 tsp (5 ml) salt

- Heat the oil or ghee in a medium-sized heavy-based saucepan.
- Add the chili and ginger followed by the hing.
- Fold in the potatoes, spinach and salt. Gently simmer over a low heat for about 15 minutes or until soft.

VEGETABLE DISHES

A simple preparation that requires a basic white sauce with a hint of nutmeg.

Preparation time : 20 minutes
Serves : 4 - 6 persons

2 bunches spinach (approx 230 g) coarsely chopped
2 tbs (30 ml) butter
2 tbs (30 ml) flour
2 cups (500 ml) milk
¼ tsp (1,2 ml) nutmeg
¼ tsp (1,2 ml) hing
¼ tsp (1,2 ml) black pepper
1 tsp (5 ml) salt

• Steam the spinach in as little water as possible, then drain.
• Melt the butter in a medium-sized heavy-based saucepan.

• Braise the flour in the butter.
• Whisk in the milk, nutmeg, hing and black pepper, stirring continuously as it thickens.
• Fold in the spinach and salt.

Serving suggestion : Serve as part of a Western meal, which may include steamed pumpkin, green peas and roasted potatoes.

* *Variation : Add small squares of curd (115 g) made from 1 litre full cream milk.*

Grandpa's Barbeque Vegetables

A family gathering for Sunday lunch where the food is cooked out-doors over a grill, is the perfect time to try this special dish.

Preparation time : 10 minutes
Roasting time : 30 minutes
Serves : 4 - 6 persons

1 large eggplant
1 small ripe papaya
1 small green pepper
2 large green chilies
1 tsp (5 ml) salt
¼ tsp (1,2 ml) black pepper
3 tbs (45 ml) olive oil
1 tbs (15 ml) finely chopped fresh mint.

• Wrap the vegetables in aluminium foil and roast on the outdoor fire until tender.
• Peel and mash.
• Fold in salt, black pepper, olive oil and mint.

Serving suggestion : Serve with vegetable kebabs, roasted corn, potato salad and French bread.

Mixed Vegetable Stew

Brighten up a vegetable dish with rounds of whole yellow sweet corn.

Preparation time : 30 minutes
Serves : 4 - 6 persons

2 tbs (30 ml) oil or ghee
¼ tsp (1,2 ml) mustard seeds
½ tsp (2,5 ml) cumin seeds
¼ tsp (1,2 ml) fenugreek seeds
4 - 6 curry leaves
1 tsp (5 ml) finely grated fresh ginger
One whole yellow sweet corn cut into 2 cm discs
1 small cauliflower (approx 200 g) cut into
medium-sized florets
2 medium potatoes (approx 230 g) peeled and diced
into about 2 cm cubes
1 medium carrot cut into small rounds
½ cup (125 ml) freshly boiled or frozen green peas
¼ tsp (1,2 ml) hing
½ tsp (2,5 ml) coriander powder
½ tsp (2,5 ml) cayenne pepper
1 tsp (5 ml) turmeric powder
1 medium tomato finely diced
1 tsp (5 ml) salt
1 tbs (15 ml) finely chopped fresh coriander

• Heat the oil or ghee in a medium-sized heavy-
  based saucepan.
• Add the mustard seeds and when they begin to
  splutter, add the cumin seeds and fenugreek seeds
  followed by the curry leaves and ginger.
• Fold in the vegetables except for the green peas.
• Gently simmer with the lid on, stirring
  occasionally for about 15 minutes or until three
  quarter cooked.
• Add the green peas, powdered spices, tomato
  and salt.
• Cook for another 10 minutes until the vegetables
  are tender yet crisp.
• Garnish with coriander.

*Variation: Use broccoli, squash and green beans as
  substitutes for any of the vegetables.*

Mixed Vegetables in Spicy White Sauce

Try this oriental creamy white sauce curry with steamed or deep-fried mixed vegetables.

Preparation time : 30 minutes
Serves : 4 - 6 persons

For the vegetables use 500 g of any combination
of the following : cauliflower, broccoli, green beans,
peas, potatoes, eggplants, pumpkin, squash, patty pans,
chou chou, calabash or carrots.

• Lightly salt the vegetables and steam with as little
  water as possible or for a richer taste, lightly salt
  and deep-fry until soft yet crisp.

For the Sauce
2 tbs (30 ml) butter
¼ tsp (1,2 ml) mustard seeds
¼ tsp (1,2 ml) cumin seeds
¼ tsp (1,2 ml) fenugreek seeds
1 chili finely chopped (optional)
½ tsp (2,5 ml) finely grated ginger

1 tsp (5 ml) fresh thyme
¼ tsp (1,2 ml) hing
2 tbs (30 ml) flour
2 cups (500 ml) milk
½ tsp (2,5 ml) salt
1 tbs (15 ml) finely chopped fresh coriander

• Melt the butter in a medium-sized heavy-based
  saucepan.
• Add the mustard seeds and when they begin to
  splutter, add the cumin seeds and fenugreek seeds
  followed by the chili, ginger, thyme and hing.
• Add the flour to the spices and braise.
• Whisk in the milk and salt. Stir continuously
  as the mixture thickens.
• Fold in the vegetables.
• Garnish with coriander.

Vegetarian 'Fish'
(Kiroch)

Homemade Cheese
in Cream Sauce (Malai Panir)

Vegetarian 'Fish' (Kiroch)

Large patta leaves are the traditional vegetable for this preparation. However, in most Western countries they are not so readily available and can be replaced by 2 large spinach leaves.

Preparation time : 45 minutes
Makes : 10 pieces

Use 1 cup (250 ml) of yellow split pea dhal. Soak for at least 3 hours, drain and crush in a food processor. (Do not add water.) Add ¼ cup (60 ml) chickpea flour. Keep about 2 tablespoons (30 ml) of this dhal paste aside for the sauce.
or
2 cups (500 ml) chickpea flour and ½ cup (125 ml) water mixed together to make a thick paste.

1 chili finely chopped
½ tsp (2,5 ml) hing
1 tsp (5 ml) turmeric powder
1 tbs (15 ml) curry powder or masala
1 tsp (5 ml) salt
2 large patta leaves

- Add the chili, hing, turmeric powder, curry powder or masala and salt to the chickpea paste.
- Remove the thick part of the stalk of the patta leaves.
- Spread half the paste evenly over one of the leaves, then place the remaining leaf on top. Spread the rest of the paste on top of the last leaf. (Photo 1&2)
- Roll up like a Swiss roll and place in a steamer for about 15 minutes or until firm.
- Allow to cool and cut into 2 cm discs.
- Deep-fry until crisp, then drain in a colander.

For the Sauce
1 tbs (15 ml) oil or ghee
1 chili finely chopped (optional)
4 - 6 curry leaves
½ tsp (2,5 ml) finely grated ginger
¼ tsp (1,2 ml) hing
1 medium tomato finely diced
3 tbs (45 ml) curry powder or masala
4 cups (1000 ml) water
1 tsp (5 ml) salt
2 tbs (30 ml) dhal paste kept from the above
or 2 tbs (30 ml) chickpea flour mixed with a little water to form a paste
1 tbs (15 ml) finely chopped fresh coriander

- Heat the oil or ghee in a medium-sized heavy-based saucepan.
- Add the chili, curry leaves, ginger and hing.
- Add the tomato and sauté until soft and velvety.
- Add the curry powder or masala, water, salt and dhal paste
- Bring to a gentle boil and simmer for about 10 minutes, stirring occasionally as the sauce thickens.
- Fold in the vegetarian fish and garnish with coriander.

* *Variation: Tomato sauce can be used instead of curry or masala sauce.*

Sweet and Sour Vegetables

The vegetables, fruit and nuts in this recipe are a prefect combination for this tangy, succulent, sweet and sour curry.

Preparation time : 30 minutes
Serves : 4 - 6 persons

1 small cauliflower (approx 200 g) cut into medium-sized florets
1 small eggplant (approx 100 g) diced into about 1 ½ cm cubes
1 medium carrot diced into about 1 cm cubes
A few green beans (approx 50 g) halved, then cut into about 1 ½ cm diagonal slices
1 medium potato (approx 115 g) peeled and diced into about 1 ½ cm cubes
1 small pineapple (approx 100 g) peeled and diced into about 1 ½ cm cubes
½ green pepper cut into thin strips
115 g curd made from 1 litre full cream milk, diced into about 1 ½ cm cubes
¼ cup (60 ml) blanched almonds
1 tbs (15 ml) oil or ghee
½ tsp (2,5 ml) cumin seeds
1 chili finely chopped
½ tsp (2,5 ml) finely grated fresh ginger
1 tsp (5 ml) turmeric powder
1 tsp (5 ml) paprika
½ tsp (2,5 ml) garam masala (optional)
¼ tsp (1,2ml) hing
1 ½ tsp (7,5 ml) salt
1 tbs (15 ml) tamarind
½ cup (125 ml) water
½ cup (125 ml) sugar
1 tbs (15 ml) finely chopped fresh coriander

- Separately deep-fry all the vegetables and fruit until soft yet crisp.
- Deep-fry the curd until golden brown, then drain and soak in lightly salted warm whey until plump.
- Deep-fry the almonds until golden brown.
- Heat the oil or ghee in a medium-sized heavy-based saucepan and fry the cumin seeds followed by the chili and ginger.
- Fold in the vegetables, fruit, nuts, curd, turmeric powder, paprika, garam masala, hing and salt.
- Soak the tamarind in the water and strain from pips.
- Add the tamarind water to the curry along with the sugar. Simmer over a low heat for about 5 minutes so that the flavours can be absorbed.
- Garnish with coriander.

Vegetarian 'Eggs'

These resemble eggs but are made with homemade cheese and mash potato.

Preparation time : 30 minutes
Makes : 6 large rounds

4 medium potatoes (approx 460 g) boiled, peeled and mashed
1 ½ tsp (7,5 ml) salt
¼ tsp (1,2 ml) black pepper
¼ tsp (1,2 ml) hing
1 tbs (15 ml) finely chopped fresh coriander or parsley
2 tbs (30 ml) butter
115 g curd made from 1 litre milk
½ tbs (7,5 ml) oil or ghee
1 small cinnamon stick (approx 3 cm)
½ tsp (2,5 ml) turmeric powder
¼ cup (60 ml) semolina

- Fold 1 teaspoon (5 ml) of the salt, black pepper, hing, coriander or parsley and butter into the mash potato.
- Knead the curd until smooth.
- Heat the oil or ghee in a small frying pan.
- Add the cinnamon stick, turmeric powder, curd and remaining salt. Mix well and cook for a few moments.

- Allow to cool.
- Roll into 6 balls.
- Divide the mash potato into 6 parts and mould around the curd balls so that you have 6 large 'eggs'.
- Coat each 'egg' with semolina and deep-fry in moderate hot oil, two at a time, for a few seconds until golden brown and crisp, then drain. Only the outer layer needs to be fried.

Serving suggestion : Cut each 'egg' in half and serve with cooked tomato chutney and garnish with fresh coriander.

* Variations : Instead of using semolina make pakora batter (see page 91) to coat the eggs. Deep-fry in the same way.

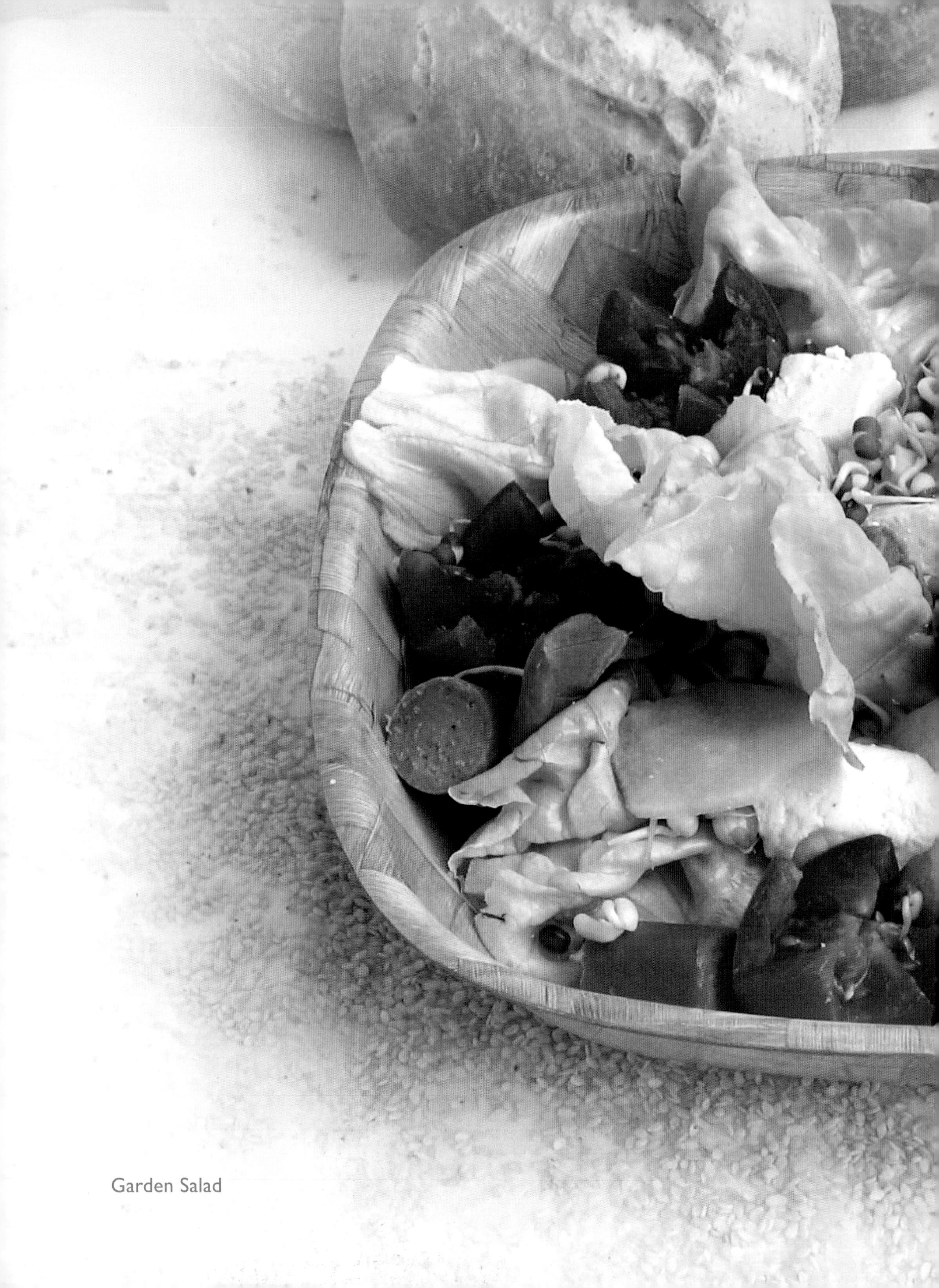

Garden Salad

Salads and
Salad dressings

✺ SALADS & SALAD DRESSINGS ✺

Steamed Beetroot, Potato and Carrot Salad
A wholesome and healthy salad.

Preparation time : 30 minutes
Serves : 4 - 6 persons

2 medium beetroots
3 medium potatoes
2 medium carrots
½ tsp (2,5 ml) hing
1 ½ tsp (7,5 ml) salt
½ tsp (2,5 ml) black pepper
3 tbs (45 ml) olive oil
Juice of ½ lemon
2 tbs (30 ml) finely chopped parsley

• Cover the vegetables with water and pressure-cook for 15 minutes.
• Drain and allow the vegetables to cool down.
• Peel and chop into thin slices.
• Mix the hing, salt, black pepper, olive oil and lemon juice together and fold into the vegetables.
• Garnish with parsley.

Tomato and Cucumber Salad
Serve this salad in small amounts.

Preparation time : 10 minutes
Serves : 4 persons

1 medium cucumber peeled and coarsely grated
4 medium tomatoes (approx 460 g) finely diced
2 tbs (30 ml) olive oil
1 tsp (5 ml) salt
¼ tsp (1,2 ml) black pepper

¼ tsp (1,2 ml) hing
2 tbs (30 ml) finely chopped fresh coriander

• Squeeze out excess water from the cucumber.
• Toss all the ingredients together.

Cucumber Raita
A spicy yoghurt salad that goes well with biryani or khichari.

Preparation time : 10 minutes
Serves : 4 - 6 persons

1 medium cucumber
½ cup (125 ml) yoghurt
½ tsp (2,5 ml) salt
1 tbs (15 ml) oil
¼ tsp (1,2 ml) mustard seeds
¼ tsp (1,2 ml) cumin seeds
1 green chili finely chopped
¼ tsp (1,2 ml) hing
1 tbs (15 ml) finely chopped fresh coriander

• Grate the cucumber and squeeze out excess water.
• Fold in the yoghurt and salt.
• Heat the oil in a small frying pan.
• Add the mustard seeds and when they begin to splutter, add the cumin seeds followed by the chili and hing.
• Fold into the cucumber mixture.
• Garnish with coriander..

Cole Slaw

A refreshing salad that should be kept refrigerated.

Preparation time : 10 minutes
Serves : 4 - 6 persons

1 small cabbage finely shredded
1 medium carrot coarsely grated
¼ cup (60 ml) sunflower seeds lightly toasted
1 small apple diced into small cubes
¼ cup (60 ml) mung sprouts

½ tsp (2,5 ml) salt
½ cup (125 ml) eggless mayonnaise (see page79)

• Squeeze out excess water from the cabbage.
• Toss all the ingredients together.

Garden Salad

A colourful salad for an outdoor occasion.

Preparation time : 10 minutes
Serves : 4 - 6 persons

Leaves from1 medium lettuce
½ small cucumber sliced into thin rounds
1 medium tomato cut into small wedges
1 medium carrot coarsely grated
¼ cup (60 ml) fresh corn kernels
1 soya sausage cut into small rounds

¼ cup (60 ml) mung sprouts
½ cup (125 ml) feta cheese broken into chunks

• Toss all the ingredients together. Just before
  serving fold in olive oil and lemon juice dressing
  (see page78).

Rice Salad

A lovely spicy and fruity rice salad.

Preparation time : 15 minutes
Serves : 4 - 6 persons

2 cups (500 ml) cooked rice
1 peach diced into small cubes
½ cup (125 ml) celery rounds
½ green pepper diced into small cubes
¼ cup (60 ml) sunflower seeds
¼ cup (60 ml) raisins
¼ cup (60 ml) olive oil

1 tbs (15 ml) lemon juice
½ tsp (2,5 ml) curry powder
1 tsp (5 ml) soy sauce
½ tsp (2,5 ml) honey
1 tbs (15 ml) finely chopped parsley

• Toss all the ingredients together.

Fruit Salad
Here are some suggestions as to how to serve this well known salad.

Preparation time : 10 - 15 minutes
Serves : 4 persons

1 apple diced into small cubes
2 bananas sliced into small rounds
1 guava diced into small cubes
A few grapes
A few strawberries
1 mango or papaya diced into small cubes
¼ cup (60 ml) hazel nuts (optional)

• Squeeze the juice of one orange and add
  2 tablespoons (30 ml) sugar or honey to taste.

or
• Blend the mango or papaya with 2 tablespoons
  (30 ml) sugar or honey and fold in the rest
  of the fruit & nuts.
or
• Make homemade custard (see page128)
  and use as a base for the fruit salad.
or
• Simply serve with slightly sweetened fresh
  whipped cream.

Olive Oil and Lemon Dressing
A simple salad dressing for a green salad.

Preparation time : 5 minutes
Makes : dressing for one medium salad

4 tbs (60 ml) olive oil
2 tbs (30 ml) lemon juice
Pinch of sugar
¼ tsp (1,2 ml) salt
¼ tsp (1,2 ml) black pepper
¼ tsp (1,2 ml) hing

• Whisk all the ingredients together.

Sunflower Seed Dressing
Rich in enzymes, this creamy salad dressing will enliven a simple green salad.

Preparation time : 10 minutes
Makes : dressing for one medium salad

½ cup (125 ml) toasted sunflower seeds
½ cup (125 ml) yoghurt
½ cup (125 ml) oil
1 tsp (5 ml) salt
1 tbs (15 ml) sugar
¼ cup (60 ml) lemon juice

• Blend the seeds, yoghurt, oil, salt and sugar
  together in a food processor until a creamy
  mixture forms.
• Gradually add the lemon juice until the mixture
  thickens.

Avocado Salad Dressing

When avocados are in season, try this creamy salad dressing with green salad.

Preparation time : 10 minutes
Makes : dressing for one medium salad

1 medium avocado
½ tsp (2,5 ml) salt
¼ tsp (1,2 ml) black pepper
½ tsp (2,5 ml) mixed herbs
1 tbs (15 ml) lemon juice
1 cup (250 ml) yoghurt

• Blend all the ingredients together into
  a creamy dressing.

Buttermilk Dressing

A quick and easy salad dressing with a slight reddish tinge.

Preparation time : 5 minutes
Makes : dressing for one medium salad

½ cup (125 ml) buttermilk
⅓ cup (80 ml) oil
½ tsp (2,5 ml) hing
½ tsp (2,5 ml) sugar
½ tsp (2,5 ml) paprika
1 tsp (5 ml) basil
⅓ cup (80 ml) lemon juice

• Blend the buttermilk, oil, hing, sugar, paprika
  and basil together.
• Gradually add the lemon juice until the
  mixture thickens.

Eggless Mayonnaise

An alternative mayonnaise that is quick to prepare.

Preparation time : 10 minutes
Makes : dressing for one medium salad

¾ cup (180 ml) evaporated milk, chilled
¾ cup (180 ml) salad oil
½ tsp (2,5 ml) salt
1 tbs (15 ml) sugar
1 tsp (5 ml) mustard powder
½ tsp (2,5 ml) paprika
3 tbs (45ml) lemon juice

• Blend the evaporated milk in a food processor.
• Gradually add the salad oil.
• Add the salt, sugar, mustard powder and paprika.
• Gradually add the lemon juice. The lemon juice
  will thicken the mixture to the right consistency.

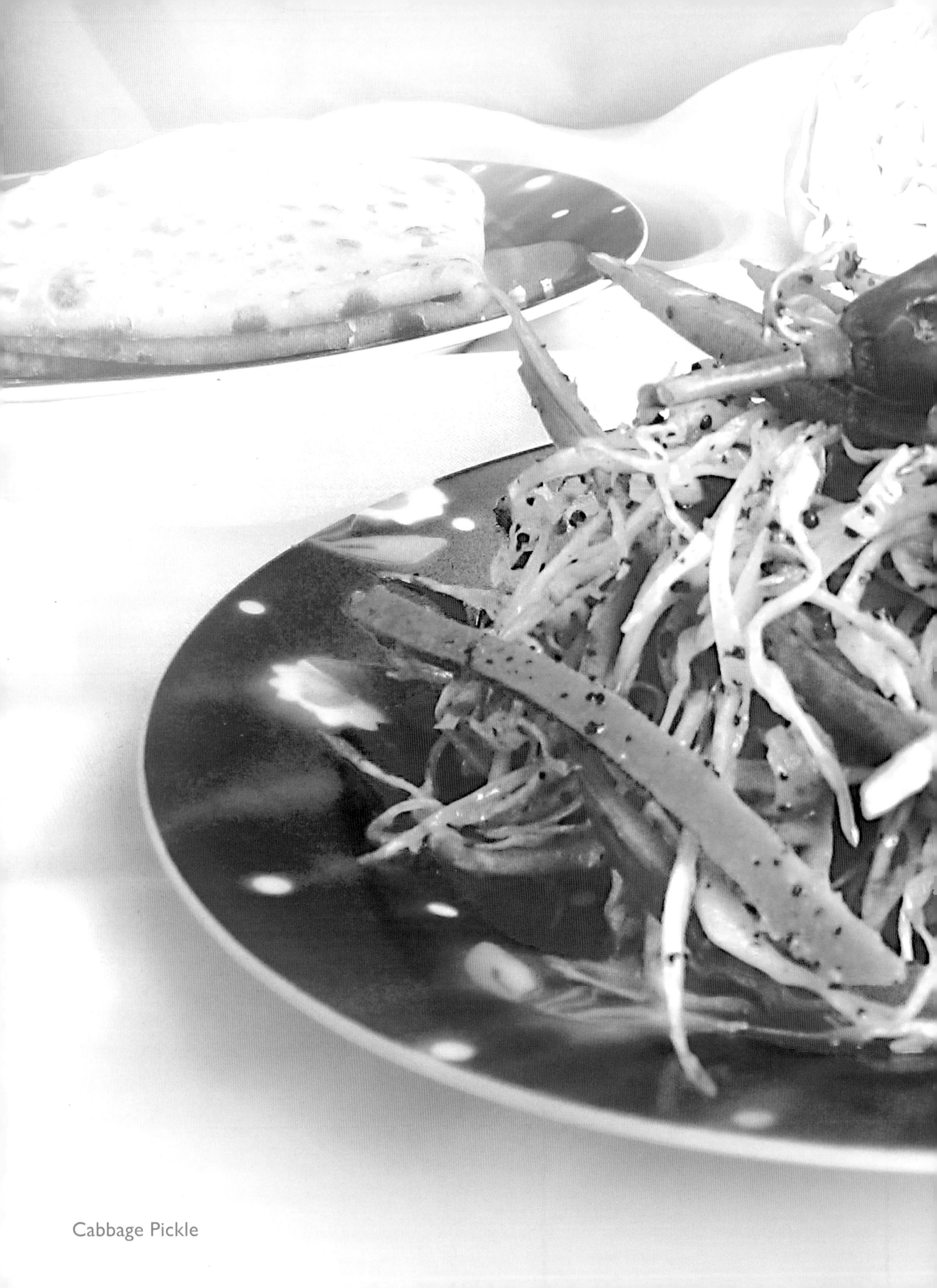

Cabbage Pickle

Condiments

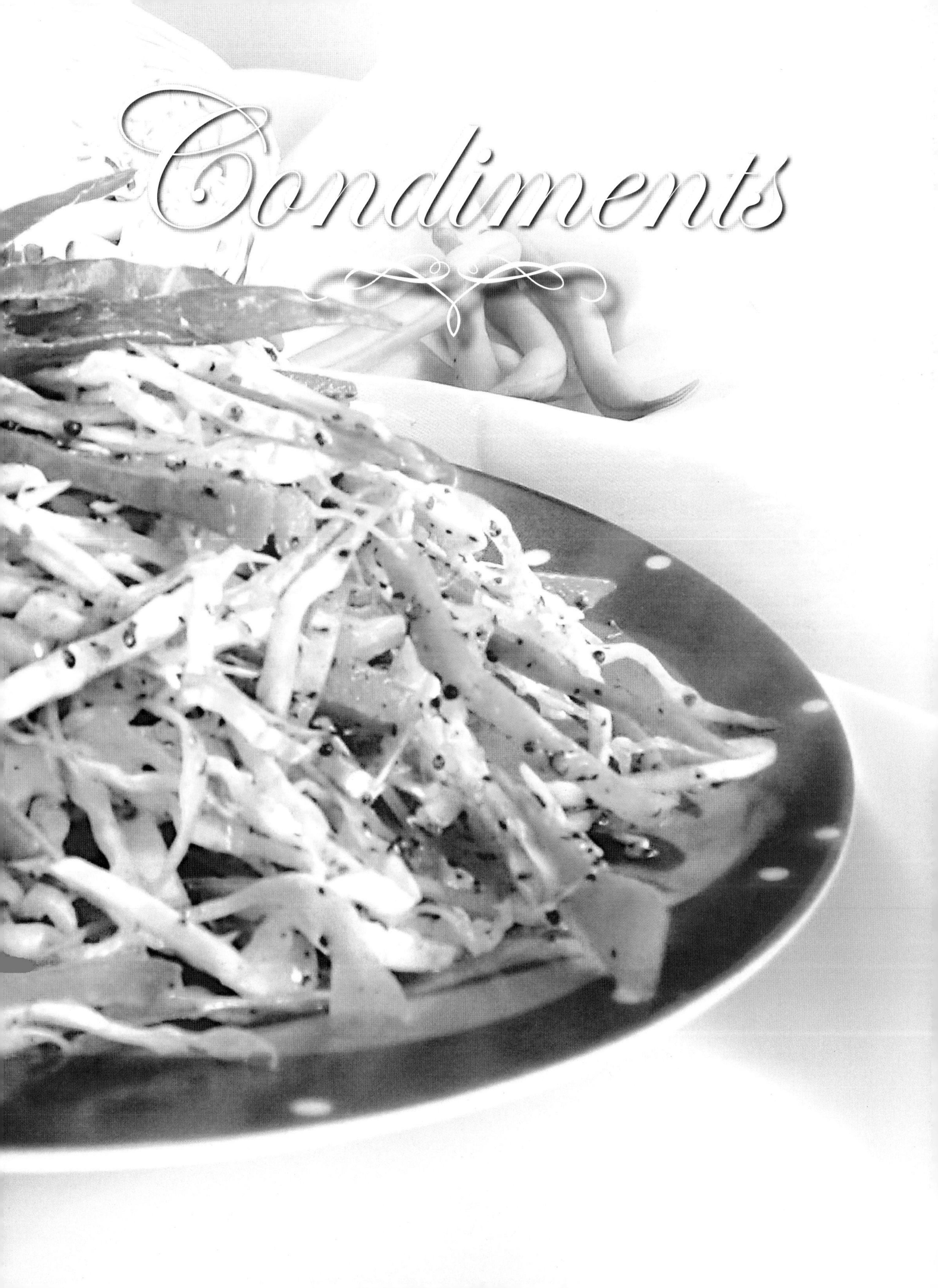

CONDIMENTS

Cabbage Pickle

A tasty accompaniment for bean curry and roti.

Preparation time : 15 minutes
Marinating time : 30 minutes

6 cups (1500 ml) finely shredded cabbage
1 cup (250 ml) long strips of thinly cut green beans
1 cup (250 ml) long strips of thinly cut carrots
1 tbs (15 ml) finely ground mustard seeds
1 tbs (15 ml) turmeric powder
½ tsp (2,5 ml) hing

3 tbs (45 ml) oil
1 tsp (5 ml) salt

• Toss all the ingredients together and allow to marinade for at least 30 minutes before serving.

Green Mango Pickle

Green mangoes are very popular for pickles. This preparation can be conveniently stored for months in a sealed container. Small amounts are usually served at meals (two to three pieces per person).

Preparation time : 10 minutes
Drying time : one sunshine day
Marinating time : one week

5 medium green mangoes
2 tsp (10 ml) salt
2 tbs (30 ml) mustard seeds
½ tsp (2,5 ml) fenugreek seeds
1 red chili
1 tbs (15 ml) turmeric powder
1 cup (250 ml) oil

• Remove the pips from the mangoes and slice into segments.

• Sprinkle with salt and place in the sunshine for one day. Alternatively dry out in a low heated oven.
• Dry roast the seeds on a griddle pan or in a small frying pan.
• Finely grind in a spice grinder along with the chili and turmeric powder.
• Coat the mangoes with the spices and oil. Place in a sealed container and store for at least one week before serving.

Green Papaya Pickle

A popular condiment made from unripe fruit, also known as achar. Can be made well in advance.

Preparation time : 10 minutes
Allow a few hours for marinating time

3 cups (750 ml) peeled and grated green papaya
4 tbs (60 ml) oil
1 ½ tsp (7,5 ml) salt
2 tbs (30 ml) freshly ground mustard seeds
1 tsp (5 ml) turmeric powder
1 chili finely chopped

• Mix all the ingredients together and allow to marinade for a few hours before serving. Keep refrigerated if kept for more than one day.

* *Variation: Use green mangoes in place of papaya. Gently pound the fruit instead of grating it.*

Fruit Chutney

This chutney can be made with apples, pineapples, ripe mangoes, peaches, plums or apricots.

Preparation time : 20 - 25 minutes

4 medium apples peeled and diced into small cubes
1 tbs (15 ml) oil or ghee
1 chili finely chopped
4 cloves
1 small cinnamon stick (approx 5 cm)
½ tsp (2,5 ml) turmeric powder
¼ tsp (1,2 ml) hing
¼ cup (60 ml) water
2 tbs (30 ml) sugar

- Heat the oil or ghee in a small heavy-based saucepan.
- Add the chili, cloves and cinnamon stick followed by the turmeric powder and hing.
- Braise the apples in the spices for a few moments, then add the water.
- Allow to gently simmer for 15 minutes until soft.
- Fold in the sugar.

Green Mango Chutney

A fresh mango chutney that is quick to prepare.

Preparation time : 10 minutes

4 medium green mangoes
1 cup (250 ml) loosely packed fresh mint
1 tsp (5 ml) salt
2 chilies

- Remove the pips from the mangoes. Place all ingredients into a food processor and blend into a smooth paste. (No need to add water.)

Raw Tomato and Fresh Mint Chutney

Fresh and easy to prepare as it requires no cooking.

Preparation time : 10 minutes

4 medium tomatoes (approx 460 g)
1 cup (250 ml) loosely packed fresh mint
1 or 2 chilies depending on taste
1 tsp (5 ml) salt

- Place all the ingredients in a food processor and blend into a smooth chutney.

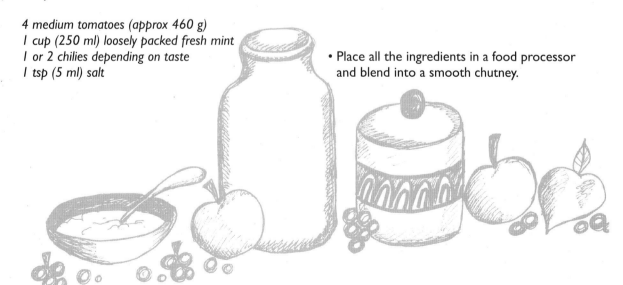

Coconut and Fresh Mint Chutney

In tropical countries coconuts are used for a variety of purposes such as for worship, cooking and in beverages. Here I have included a traditional recipe for coconut chutney. You could use commercially sold desiccated coconut, but the former is far more superior.

Preparation time : 20 minutes
Makes for a large gathering

1 whole dried coconut
1 tbs (15 ml) tamarind
2 cups (500 ml) water
1 cup (250 ml) loosely packed fresh mint
2 chilies
1 tsp (5 ml) salt

- Remove the hairy outer covering of the coconut.
- Look carefully at the hard shell of the coconut and you will see that there are three holes that appear like a monkey's face. With a sharp tool such as a screwdriver, pierce a hole in the mouth of the face and pour the coconut water out.
- Wrap the coconut in a large kitchen towel and smash it with great force against a hard surface so that the coconut breaks. If the coconut pulp does not come out easily from the shell, place the broken pieces on an open flame for a few minutes. The shell and white flesh will separate automatically. Use a tong to remove the coconut from the flame.
- Roast the coconut pulp either by placing it directly on the flame again or cut into chunks and place in an oven or grate and dry roast in a wok or heavy-based frying pan. Black spots will form and this will add to the colour and taste of the chutney.
- Soak the tamarind in ½ cup of the water. Strain from pips.
- Add all the ingredients together including the tamarind water and blend in a food processor into smooth paste.

Hint: When using desiccated coconut the amount of water will decrease. Use 1 cup (250 ml) desiccated coconut with approx 1 cup (250 ml) water.

Nut, Tamarind and Fresh Mint Chutney

A perfect chutney for fried rice.

Preparation time : 10 minutes

1 tbs (15 ml) tamarind pulp
¼ cup (60 ml) water
1 cup (250 ml) roasted peanuts (unsalted)
1 cup (250 ml) or 125 g fresh mint loosely packed
1 tsp (5 ml) salt
2 red dried chilies

- Soak the tamarind in the water and strain from pips.
- Blend all the ingredients together until creamy.

Date and Tamarind Chutney

Sweet and sour chutney goes well with vegetable fritters or samosas.

Preparation time : 20 minutes

1 tbs (15 ml) oil or ghee
¼ tsp (1,2 ml) cumin seeds
1 chili finely chopped
½ cup (125 ml) dates without seeds
2 tbs (30 ml) tamarind soaked in ¾ cup (180 ml) water and strained from pips
1 tsp (5 ml) sugar
¼ tsp (1,2 ml) salt

- Heat the oil or ghee in a small heavy-based saucepan.
- Add the cumin seeds and chili. Fry for a few moments.
- Add the dates, tamarind water, sugar and salt. Gently simmer for 15 minutes, stirring occasionally.

Cooked Tomato Chutney

This chutney can be used as a base for various vegetable dishes or can be served with your favourite savoury.

Preparation time : 20 minutes

1 tbs (15 ml) oil or ghee
¼ tsp (1,2 ml) mustard seeds
¼ tsp (1,2 ml) cumin seeds
1 chili finely chopped
½ tsp (2,5 ml) finely grated ginger
1 sprig of fresh thyme
1 small cinnamon stick (approx 2 cm)
4 medium tomatoes (approx 460 g) blanched
and puréed
¼ tsp (1,2 ml) hing
½ tsp (2,5 ml) turmeric powder
1 tsp (5 ml) salt

1 tsp (5 ml) sugar
1 tbs (15 ml) finely chopped fresh coriander

- Heat the oil or ghee in a small heavy-based saucepan.
- Add the mustard seeds and when they begin to splutter, add the cumin seeds followed by the chili, ginger, thyme and cinnamon stick.
- Add the tomato, hing and turmeric powder. Allow to simmer for 15 minutes or until well cooked.
- Mix in with salt and sugar.
- Garnish with coriander.

Eggplant Chutney

This chutney is best served as part of a meal with wholewheat pooris.

Preparation time : 10 minutes
Allow time for roasting or boiling

1 large eggplant (approx 300 g)
2 tbs (30 ml) oil or ghee
1 chili finely chopped
6 - 8 curry leaves
¼ tsp (1,2 ml) hing
1 tsp (5 ml) salt
1 tbs (15 ml) finely chopped fresh coriander

- The eggplant can either be roasted in the oven for about 30 minutes or boiled until tender.
- Peel and mash.
- Heat the oil or ghee in a medium-sized heavy-based saucepan.
- Add the mustard seeds and when they begin to splutter, add the chili, curry leaves and hing.
- Fold in the eggplant and salt.
- Garnish with coriander.

Potato Chutney

Serve this spicy mash potato with any flat bread such as wholewheat pooris or use as a filling for roti rolls.

Preparation time : 20 - 25 minutes

4 cups (1000 ml) or approx 690 g potatoes peeled
and diced into about 2 cm cubes
2 tbs (30 ml) oil or ghee
½ tsp (2,5 ml) mustard seeds
¼ tsp (1,2 ml) fenugreek seeds
2 dried whole red chilies
6 - 8 curry leaves
1 tsp (5 ml) finely grated ginger
¼ tsp (1,2) hing
1 medium tomato finely diced

1½ tsp (7,5 ml) salt
1 tbs (15 ml) finely chopped fresh coriander

- Boil the potatoes until soft, drain and mash.
- Heat the oil or ghee in a medium-sized saucepan.
- Add mustard seeds and when they begin to splutter, add the fenugreek seeds followed by the chili, curry leaves, ginger and hing.
- Add the tomato and sauté until soft and velvety.
- Fold in the mash potato, salt and coriander.

Traditional Indian Samosa,
Bread Fritters with Potato and Dhal
Filling(Chana Poori) and Homemade
Cheese Samosa

Savouries

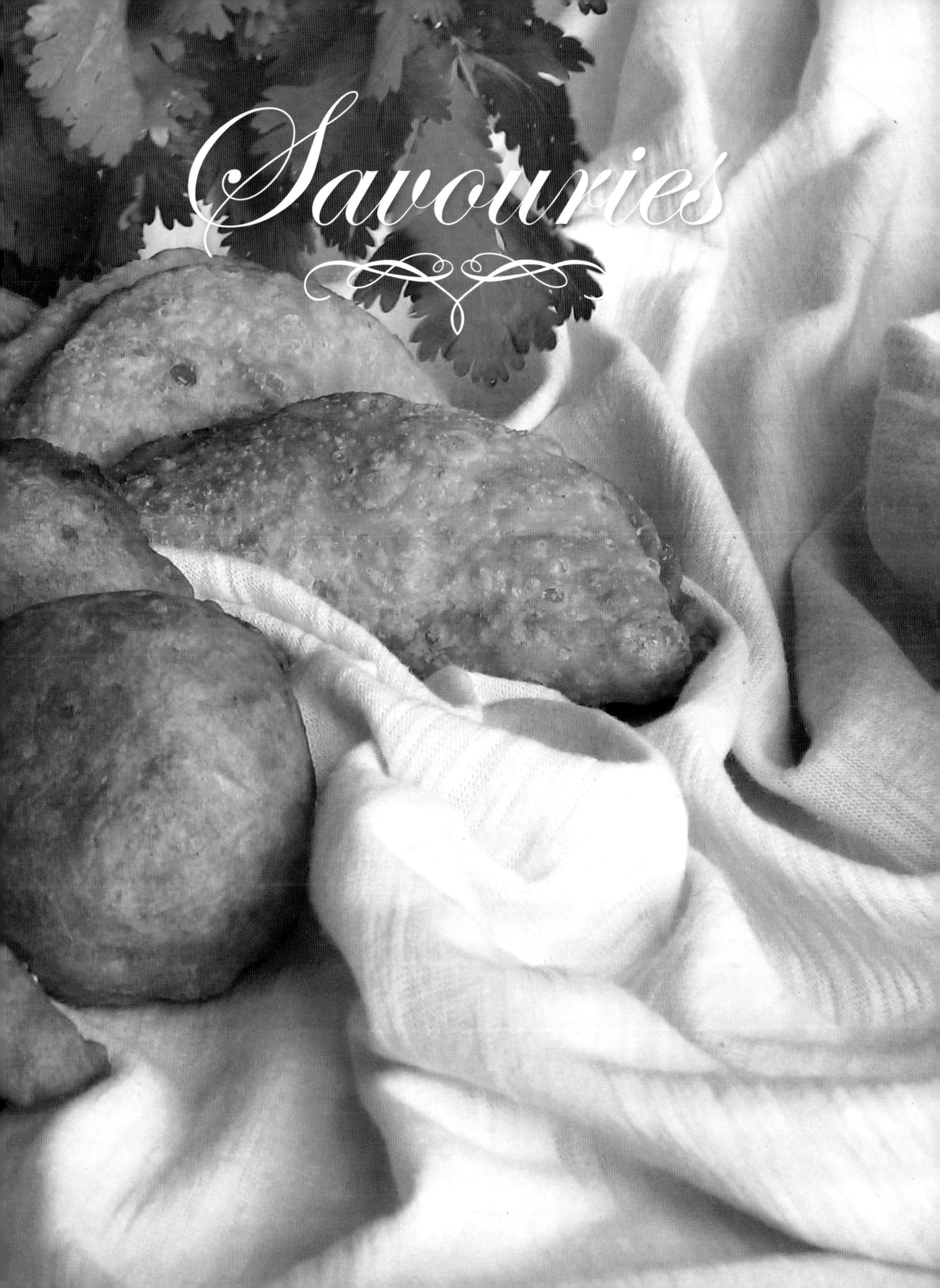

Traditional Indian Samosa
A lightly spiced samosa with potato, pea and fresh mint filling.

Preparation time : 45 minutes - 1 hour
Makes : 25 small samosas

Step One: Preparing the pastry
2 cups (500 ml) flour
¼ tsp (1,2 ml) salt
Pinch of yellow colour
Approx 1 cup (250 ml) water

Mixture to separate layers
2 tbs (30 ml) oil
2 tbs (30 ml) flour

- Sift the flour and salt together.
- Stir the yellow colour into the water. Gradually add the water to the flour mixture to form a soft pliable dough. Knead well.
- Divide the dough into 5 balls and roll out into about 12 cm rounds.
- Place the rounds on top of one another, but while you are doing this rub half a tablespoon (7,5 ml) of oil and dust with half a tablespoon (7,5 ml) of flour on both sides of each round. Do not put oil or flour on top of the last round. (illus 1)
- Roll out into about a large 30 cm by 35 cm rectangle.
- Place on an ungreased baking tray and bake in a moderate oven at 180° C or 350° F for about 10 minutes so that the dough dries slightly but is still flexible.
- Cut into 6 long strips (about 5 cm in width). Gently peel the layers apart. (illus 2)
- Wrap in a cloth until ready to use.

Step Two: Preparing the filling
2 medium potatoes (approx 230 g) peeled and diced into about 1 cm cubes
1 tbs (15 ml) oil or ghee
¼ tsp (1,2 ml) mustard seeds
¼ tsp (1,2 ml) cumin seeds
1 chili finely chopped
6 - 8 curry leaves
½ tsp (2,5 ml) finely grated ginger
½ tsp (2,5 ml) turmeric powder
¼ tsp (1,2 ml) hing
¼ cup (60 ml) freshly boiled or frozen green peas
1 tsp (5 ml) salt
1 tbs (15 ml) finely chopped fresh mint

- Boil the potatoes until soft, then drain.
- Heat oil or ghee in a medium-sized heavy-based sauce pan.
- Add the mustard seeds and when they begin to splutter, add the cumin seeds followed by the chili, curry leaves, ginger, turmeric powder and hing.
- Fold in the potatoes, peas, salt and mint.
- Allow to cool before filling the pastries.

Step Three: Assembling and frying
3 tbs (45 ml) flour
4 tbs (60 ml) water

- Make a paste with the flour and water.
- Place about 2 teaspoons (10 ml) of filling at the base of each pastry strip and fold up into triangles. Seal closed with paste. (illus 3)
- Deep-fry over moderate heat until the samosas are golden brown. Drain well.

Serving suggestion : Serve hot with tomato chutney.

Freezing : Unfried samosas can be stored in the freezer until required.

Cooking tip : The pastry can also be cut and cooked on a large griddle pan over a low heat. You will need to turn over the pastry several times while cooking to prevent it from becoming crisp.
If you prefer cooking in an oven as the recipe suggests, you can use any suitable large tray that will fit the size of the pastry. You can cut the pastry in half and bake it in two batches.

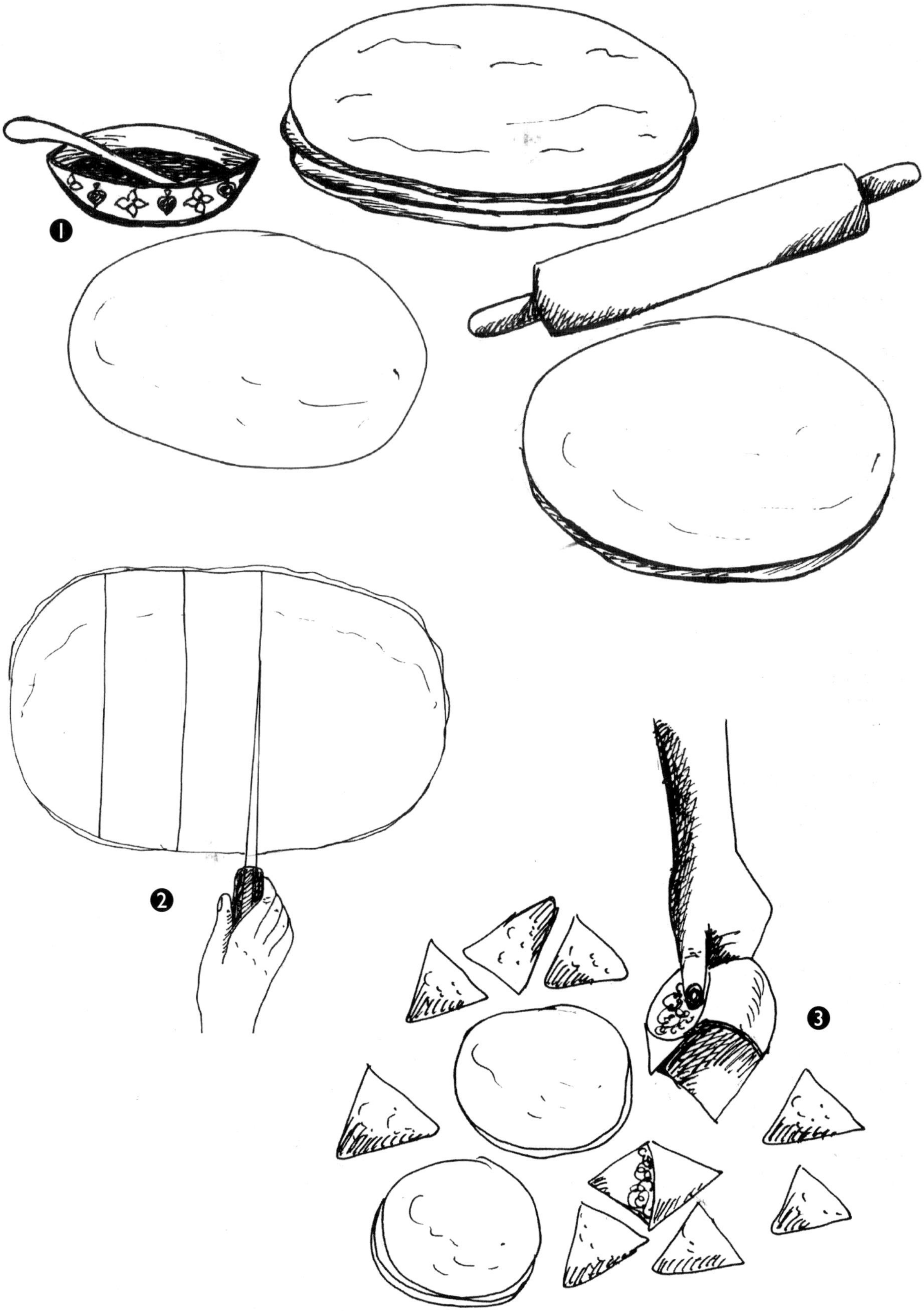
1
2
3

Homemade Cheese Samosa
A delicate samosa with curd and vegetable filling.

Preparation time : 30 minutes
Makes : 10 samosas

Step One: Preparing the pastry
1 cup (250 ml) flour
½ tsp (2,5 ml) salt
1 ½ tbs (22,5 ml) butter
Approx ½ cup (125 ml) water

- Sift the flour and salt together.
- Rub in the butter and add enough water to form a soft pliable dough.
- Cover and set aside while you prepare the filling.

Step Two: Preparing the filling
½ cup (125 ml) finely diced eggplant
(approx 0,5 cm each)
½ cup (125 ml) finely diced potatoes
(approx 0,5 cm each)
115 g curd made from 1 litre full cream milk
¼ bell pepper finely diced
1 medium tomato finely diced
1 tbs (15 ml) olive oil
½ tsp (2,5 ml) hing
½ tsp (2,5 ml) salt
1 tbs (15 ml) finely chopped fresh coriander

- Deep-fry the eggplant and potatoes, then drain.
- Crumble the curd and add the eggplant, potatoes, bell pepper and tomato.
- Fold in the olive oil, hing, salt and coriander.

Step Three: Assembling and frying
- Divide the dough into 10 balls and roll out into about 4 cm rounds.
- Place a generous amount of filling in each centre.
- Fold over the side so that you have half moon shapes and seal the sides by plaiting them or press with a fork.
- Deep-fry in moderate hot oil until golden brown.
- Drain well.

Bread Fritters with Potato and Dhal Filling (Chana Poori)

Bread-like pakora with potato and dhal filling.

Preparation time : 30 minutes
Rising time : 1 hour
Makes : 20 bite size savouries

Step One: Preparing the batter

2 cups (500 ml) flour
1 tsp (5 ml) salt
1 tbs (15 ml) instant yeast
1 tsp (5 ml) oil or ghee
¼ tsp (1,2 ml) hing
1 tbs (15 ml) finely chopped fresh coriander
Approx 1½ cups (375 ml) warm water

• Sift the flour and salt together.
• Stir in the yeast, oil or ghee, hing and coriander.
• Add enough water to form a thick batter.
• Cover and allow to rise in a warm place for about 1 hour or until double.

Step Two: Preparing the filling

½ cup (125 ml) yellow split pea dhal preferably soaked for at least 3 hours or overnight, then drained
1 cup (250 ml) small potato cubes (about 1 cm each)
2 tbs (30 ml) oil or ghee
½ tsp (2,5 ml) mustard seeds
4 - 6 curry leaves finely chopped
1 chili finely chopped
½ tsp (5 ml) turmeric powder
¼ tsp (1,2 ml) hing
½ tsp (2,5 ml) salt

• Boil the dhal and the potatoes until soft. Drain the water.
• Heat the oil or ghee in a small heavy-based saucepan.
• Add the mustard seeds and when they begin to splutter, add the curry leaves and chili followed by the turmeric powder and hing.
• Fold in the potatoes, dhal and salt.

Step Three: Assembling and frying

• Form the potato and dhal mixture into 20 small balls.
• Lightly oil your hands. Dip each ball one by one into the batter making sure they are well coated and gently drop into moderate hot oil. Deep-fry until golden brown and crisp.
• Drain well.

Broccoli Fritters (Pakoras)

Although I have used broccoli, try other vegetables such as potato, cauliflower, butternut, beetroot, spinach or zucchini.

Preparation time : 20 minutes
Makes : approx 12 pieces

¾ cup (180 ml) flour
¼ cup (60 ml) chickpea flour
1 tsp (5 ml) salt
¼ tsp (1,2 ml) hing
½ tsp (2,5 ml) turmeric powder
1 finely diced chili (optional)
1 tbs (15 ml) finely chopped fresh coriander
Approx ¾ cup (180 ml) water
1 medium broccoli (approx 230 g) cut into medium-sized florets

• Sift the flour, chickpea flour and salt together.
• Add the hing, turmeric powder, chili, coriander and enough water to form a medium batter of dropping constituency.
• Dip the vegetable pieces one by one in the batter and coat them well. Deep-fry in moderate hot oil until golden brown and crisp.
• Drain well.

Serving suggestion: Serve with chutney.

Vegetable Rolls

These savouries have a beautiful spiral form. You can select any combination of vegetables to equal at least two cups when grated.

Preparation time : 30 minutes
Makes : 16 pieces

Step One: Preparing the filling

1 tbs (15 ml) oil or ghee
½ tsp (2,5 ml) mustard seeds
1 chili finely chopped (optional)
6 - 8 curry leaves finely chopped
1 tsp (5 ml) ginger
¼ tsp (1,2 ml) hing
1 medium potato (approx 115 g) peeled and grated
1 medium carrot grated
1 cup (250 ml) or approx 50 g cabbage grated
½ tsp (2,5 ml) salt

• Heat the oil or ghee in a medium-sized heavy-based saucepan.
• Add the mustard seeds and when they begin to splutter, add the chili, curry leaves, ginger and hing.
• Mix in the vegetables and salt. Stir-fry until the mixture holds together.
• Allow to cool.

Step Two: Preparing the dough

2 cups (500 ml) flour
1 tsp (5 ml) salt
1 tsp (5 ml) turmeric powder

1 tbs (15 ml) finely chopped fresh coriander
2 tbs (30 ml) butter
Approx ¾ cup (180 ml) water

• Sift the flour, salt and turmeric powder together.
• Mix in the coriander and rub in the butter.
• Add enough water to form a soft pliable dough.
• On a lightly floured surface, roll out the dough into about a large 30 cm by 40 cm rectangle.
• Spread the filling evenly on top.
• Roll into a long Swiss roll and cut into 16 discs (about 2 ½ cm thick each).
• Gently press each disc with the palms of your hands to flatten them slightly.
• Deep-fry in moderate hot oil until golden brown and crisp.
• Drain well.

* Variations: Use eggplant chutney or ½ the recipe of the potato chutney as a filling (see page 85).

Hint: Dust the discs with some flour to prevent the savoury from opening up while frying.

Dhal Patties (Gateau Piment)

These spicy savouries are available hot on the spot at many Asian food courts in Mauritius.

Preparation time : 30 minutes
Soaking time : 3 hour
Make : 18 small patties

1 cup (250 ml) yellow split pea dhal soaked for at least 3 hours, then drained
1 tsp (5 ml) salt
¼ tsp (1,2 ml) hing
8 - 10 curry leaves
2 tbs (30 ml) finely chopped fresh coriander
2 chilies finely chopped

• Crush the dhal into a smooth paste using a food processor. (Do not add water.)

• Add the rest of the ingredients and mix well.
• Taking one tablespoon (15 ml) at a time, roll into about 18 balls, flatten and make a slight dent in each centre.
• Deep-fry in moderate hot oil until golden brown and crisp.
• Drain well.

Serving suggestion: Great as party snacks, serve these patties on cocktail sticks with fresh mint and tomato chutney.

* Variations: For a milder version, decrease the amount of chilies.

Potato and Sago Patties

A tasty potato patty that is wheat-free.

Preparation time : 30 minutes
Soaking time : 1 hour
Makes : 16 small patties

½ cup (125 ml) sago
2 potatoes (approx 460 g) boiled with the skin
1 small chili finely chopped (optional)
6 - 8 curry leaves finely chopped
2 tbs (30 ml) finely chopped fresh coriander or parsley
2 tsp (10 ml) salt

• Soak the sago for at least 1 hour until soft,
  then drain.
• Peel and mash the potatoes.

• Add the sago, chili, curry leaves, coriander
  or parsley and salt. Mix well.
• Form into 16 small patties.
• Deep-fry in small batches in hot oil until golden
  brown and crisp.
• Drain well.

Serving suggestion : Serve hot with peanut and mint
chutney.

Soya Patties

*These patties can be used to make vegetarian burgers. Place between soft rolls
with salad and a sauce of your choice.*

Preparation time : 30 minutes
Makes : 6 patties

2 cups (500 ml) or 100 g soya chunks
½ cup (125 ml) flour
½ cup (125 ml) oats
1 tsp (5 ml) salt
¼ tsp (1,2 ml) black pepper
¼ tsp (1,2 ml) hing
1 tsp (5 ml) freshly ground coriander seeds
1 tsp (5 ml) freshly ground cumin seeds
1 tbs (15 ml) finely chopped parsley

• Boil the soya until soft, drain and squeeze
  out excess water.
• Mince in a food processor. (Do not add
  any extra water.)
• Mix in the rest of the ingredients.
• Form into 6 large patties and deep-fry
  until golden brown and crisp.
• Drain well.

Mixed Vegetable Patties

A suitable patty for vegetarian burgers.

Preparation time : 30 minutes
Makes : 6 large patties

3 cups (750 ml) of mixed grated vegetables (carrots,
cabbage, chou chou, beet root or potatoes etc)
1 cup (250 ml) chickpea flour
1 tsp (5 ml) baking powder
1 tsp (5 ml) salt
¼ tsp (1,2 ml) hing
½ tsp (2,5 ml) turmeric powder

1 chili finely chopped (optional)
1 tsp (5 ml) fresh thyme

• Squeeze out excess water from the vegetables.
• Mix in the rest of the ingredients.
• Form into 6 large patties and deep-fry
  until golden brown and crisp.
• Drain well.

SAVOURIES

Baked Spinach Blocks

A Gujarati savoury with coconut and sesame seeds.

Preparation time : 30 minutes
Baking time : 30 minutes
Makes : approx 12 pieces

1 bunch spinach (approx 115 g) finely shredded
1 cup (250 ml) chickpea flour
½ cup (125 ml) flour
½ cup (125 ml) rice flour
1 tsp (5 ml) salt
1 tsp (5 ml) baking powder
½ tsp (2,5 ml) sugar
2 tsp (10 ml) lemon juice
½ tsp (2,5 ml) turmeric powder
1 tsp (5 ml) ground coriander
1 tsp (5 ml) ground cumin
1 tbs (15 ml) coconut
1 chili finely chopped
½ tsp (2,5 ml) finely grated ginger
1 tsp (5 ml) oil
1 cup (250 ml) plain yoghurt
1 tbs (15 ml) sesame seeds

- Mix all the ingredients together except for the sesame seeds.
- Spread into a lightly greased baking tray (approx 15 cm by 24 cm) and sprinkle with the sesame seeds.
- Bake in a preheated moderate oven at 180° C or 350° F for about 30 minutes or until firm.
- Cut into squares and deep-fry until golden brown and crisp.
- Drain well.

* *Variations : Use grated zucchini or cabbage in place of spinach.*

Steamed Dhal Cakes (Dokla)

This savoury cake is popular amongst the Gujarati people. It requires steaming as its method of cooking.

Preparation time : 20 minutes
Steaming time : 30 minutes
Makes : 12 pieces

3 cups (750 ml) semolina
½ tsp (2,5 ml) salt
½ tsp (2,5 ml) ginger crushed into a fine paste
½ tsp (2,5 ml) turmeric powder
1 chili finely chopped
3 tbs (45 ml) oil
2 cups (500 ml) yoghurt
½ tsp (2,5 ml) baking powder
3 tsp (15 ml) fruit salts

- Mix all the ingredients together adding the baking powder and fruit salts last.
- Spoon into a lightly greased steamer and steam for about 30 minutes or until firm.
- Remove from the container and cut into diagonal shapes.
- Prepare the garnish.

For the garnish
1 tbs (15 ml) oil
1 tbs (15 ml) sesame seeds
1 tbs (15 ml) coconut
1 tbs (15 ml) finely chopped fresh coriander
¼ tsp (1,2 ml) salt

- Heat the oil in a small saucepan.
- Braise the sesame seeds and coconut until light golden brown.
- Remove from the heat and fold in the coriander and salt.
- Spread on top of the cake.

Serving suggestion : Serve as party snacks or to accompany an oriental dinner.

Mexican Tacos

Famous Mexican bread that is served with a layer of bean curry followed by avocado dressing, sour cream and topped with grated cheese.

Preparation time : 30 minutes
Makes : 8 breads

1 ½ cups (375 ml) wholewheat flour
1 cup (250 ml) cornflour
1 tsp (5 ml) salt
Pinch of yellow food colour
2 tbs (30 ml) oil
Approx ¾ cup (180 ml) water

- Sift the flours, salt and food colour together.
- Rub in the oil and add enough water to form a soft pliable dough.

- Divide the dough into 12 balls.
- Roll out on a lightly floured surface into about 10 cm rounds.
- Shallow fry on both sides until crisp and golden brown.
- Drain well.

* *Variations: The rolled out dough can also be cut into triangles and fried as corn chips. You can also add more spices to the dough such as cayenne pepper and paprika.*

Potato Sev

Serve as a non-grain snack.

Preparation time : 15 minutes
Serves : 4 persons

4 medium potatoes (approx 460 g) peeled and coarsely grated
Drop of red food colour (optional)
Drop of green food colour (optional)
¼ cup (60 ml) raw nuts lightly salted
4 - 6 curry leaves
½ tsp (2,5 ml) salt

- Colour one quarter of the potatoes red and another quarter green.
- Deep-fry the potatoes in small batches until crisp and golden brown, then drain well.
- Deep-fry the nuts until golden brown, then drain.
- Fry the curry leaves until crisp, then drain.
- Mix the nuts and curry leaves with the potato crisps.
- Sprinkle with salt.

Banana Chips

Green bananas made into thin crisp chips.

Preparation time : 20 - 25 minutes
Serves : 4 persons (makes approx 100 g)

4 large green bananas, rinsed, peeled and cut into thin strips with a potato peeler, as you would do when making potato crisps.
4 - 6 curry leaves
¼ tsp (1,2 ml) salt

- Deep-fry the banana in small batches at a time until golden brown and crisp, then drain well.
- Deep-fry the curry leaves until crisp. Drain and gently mix with the bananas.
- Sprinkle with salt.

Sevian Noodles

A special machine for sev is necessary for making these thread-like noodles,
available at oriental grocery stores. These make fantastic snacks for parties and gatherings.

Preparation time : 20 - 30 minutes
Makes : 250 g

2 cups (500 ml) chickpea flour
1 ½ tsp (7,5 ml) salt
1 tsp (5 ml) turmeric powder
¼ tsp (1,2 ml) hing
1 tsp (5 ml) ajwain seeds finely crushed (optional)
Approx ½ cup (125 ml) water
½ cup (125 ml) raw nuts
8 - 10 curry leaves

- Sift the flour, salt, turmeric powder and hing together.
- Stir in the ajwain seeds.
- Add enough water to form a thick batter.
- Press the batter through a lightly oiled sevian machine into hot oil and deep-fry until light golden brown and crisp.
- Drain well.
- Lightly salt the nuts and deep-fry until golden brown, then drain.
- Fry the curry leaves until crisp, then drain.
- Mix the nuts and curry leaves with the sevian noodles.

Sevian Noodles

Non-Grain Pancakes

For people who are have wheat allergies, these savouries are a perfect substitute for white flour pancakes.

Preparation time : 30 minutes
Makes : 8 pancakes

1 cup (250 ml) full cream milk powder
½ cup (125 ml) starch
½ tsp (2,5 ml) salt
½ tbs (7,5 ml) butter or ghee
¾ cup (180 ml) water

• Sift the milk powder, starch and salt together.
• Rub in the butter or ghee and add enough water to form a pouring batter.
• Heat a blob of butter in a medium-sized heavy-based frying pan and pour in about three tablespoons (45 ml) of batter.
• With the aid of a back of a spoon spread the batter into a large round.
• Once the underneath is speckled brown loosen the sides, turn over and cook on the other side. The cooking should be done over a fairly low heat, as the pancake tends to brown quickly.
• Repeat the process until all the batter is used up.

Serving suggestion : Roll up with a simple potato curry and serve with tomato chutney.

Variations : For a sweet pancake, decrease the salt and add 1 tablespoon (15 ml) sugar.

Spring Rolls

Here is a simple vegetarian version of Chinese spring rolls.

Preparation time : 30 minutes
Makes : 10 spring rolls

Step one : Preparing the filling
2 tbs (30 ml) olive oil
1 tsp (5 ml) finely grated ginger
½ tsp (2,5 ml) hing
4 cups (1000 ml) finely shredded cabbage
1 medium carrot cut into thin matchstick size strips
½ cup (125 ml) small cauliflower florets
(approx 1 cm in size)
¼ green pepper coarsely grated
½ cup (125 ml) bamboo shoots
1 tsp (5 ml) salt
1 tbs (15 ml) finely chopped fresh coriander

• Heat the olive oil in a medium-sized wok.
• Add the ginger and hing followed by the vegetables and stir-fry until tender yet crisp.
• Fold in the salt and coriander.
• Allow the filling to cool down.

Step two : Assembling and frying
1 tbs (15 ml) flour
2 tbs (30 ml) water
10 pieces phyllo pastry

• Make a paste with the flour and water.
• Separate 10 sheets of phyllo pastry and spread on a working surface.
• Place a generous amount of filling the centre of each pastry.
• Tuck in the sides and roll up securing the edges with the flour paste.
• Deep-fry in moderate hot oil for a few minutes until golden brown.
• Drain well.

Serving suggestion : Serve with date and tamarind chutney or soy sauce.

Asparagus and Tomato Quiche
Here is a pure vegetarian version of this lovely dish.

Preparation time : 20 minutes
Baking time : 45 minutes
Serves : 4 persons

Step one: Preparing the base
1 cup (250 ml) flour
¼ tsp (1,2 ml) salt
1 tbs (15 ml) butter
Approx ¼ cup (60 ml) water

• Sift the flour and salt together.
• Rub in the butter and add enough water to form
  a soft dough.
• Line a small lightly greased pie dish (about 15 cm
  in diametre) with the dough.
• Blind bake in a preheated moderate oven at 180°
  C or 350° F for about 10 minutes.

Step two: Preparing the filling
1¼ cup (310 ml) milk
2 tbs (30 ml) cornflour
1 tbs (15 ml) flour
½ tsp (2,5 ml) salt
¼ tsp (1,2 ml) black pepper
½ cup (125 ml) grated cheese

• Bring one cup (250 ml) of the milk to a gentle
  boil and allow to simmer.
• Make a paste with the cornflour, flour and
  remaining milk.
• Add to the simmering milk along with the salt
  and black pepper. Keep stirring until thick.

• Fold in the cheese.

Step three: Assembling and baking
½ can (135 g) asparagus
½ cup (125 ml) grated cheese
1 medium tomato cut into thin slices
Paprika
1 sprig of rosemary

• Line the pastry base with asparagus.
• Pour over the cheese sauce.
• Sprinkle with cheese.
• Decorate with tomato slices, paprika and
  rosemary.
• Continue baking for about 30 minutes
  or until the sides of the pastry is well cooked
  and the cheese melted with speckles of golden
  brown colour.
• Allow to set before serving.

Savoury Pancakes

Pancakes are so versatile that they can be prepared using different combinations of flours, served sweet or rolled up with savoury fillings. In this recipe I have suggested wholewheat flour for a healthy version and have added vegetables and seasoning to the batter.

Preparation time : 30 minutes
Makes : 8 pancakes

2 cups (500 ml) wholewheat flour
1 tsp (5 ml) salt
¼ tsp (1,2 ml) hing
1 cup (250 ml) or 50 g finely shredded cabbage
1 medium tomato finely diced into small cubes
1 tbs (15 ml) finely chopped parsley
Approx 2 cups (500 ml) water

- Sift the flour, salt and hing together.
- Fold in the rest of the ingredients adding enough water to form a thin batter.
- Heat a small blob of butter in a medium-sized frying pan.
- Pour approx 4 tablespoons (60 ml) of batter into the pan and spread evenly into a large round with the help of the back of a tablespoon.
- Once the underneath is speckled brown loosen the sides, turn over and cook on the other side.
- Repeat the process until all the batter is used up.

Serving suggestion : Serve hot for breakfast with yogi tea.

* *Variations : Use finely shredded spinach in place of the cabbage. Freshly chopped coriander or thyme can be used instead of parsley. For those who like spicier pancake, add some chilies.*

Pasta Dishes

Stir-Fried Noodles

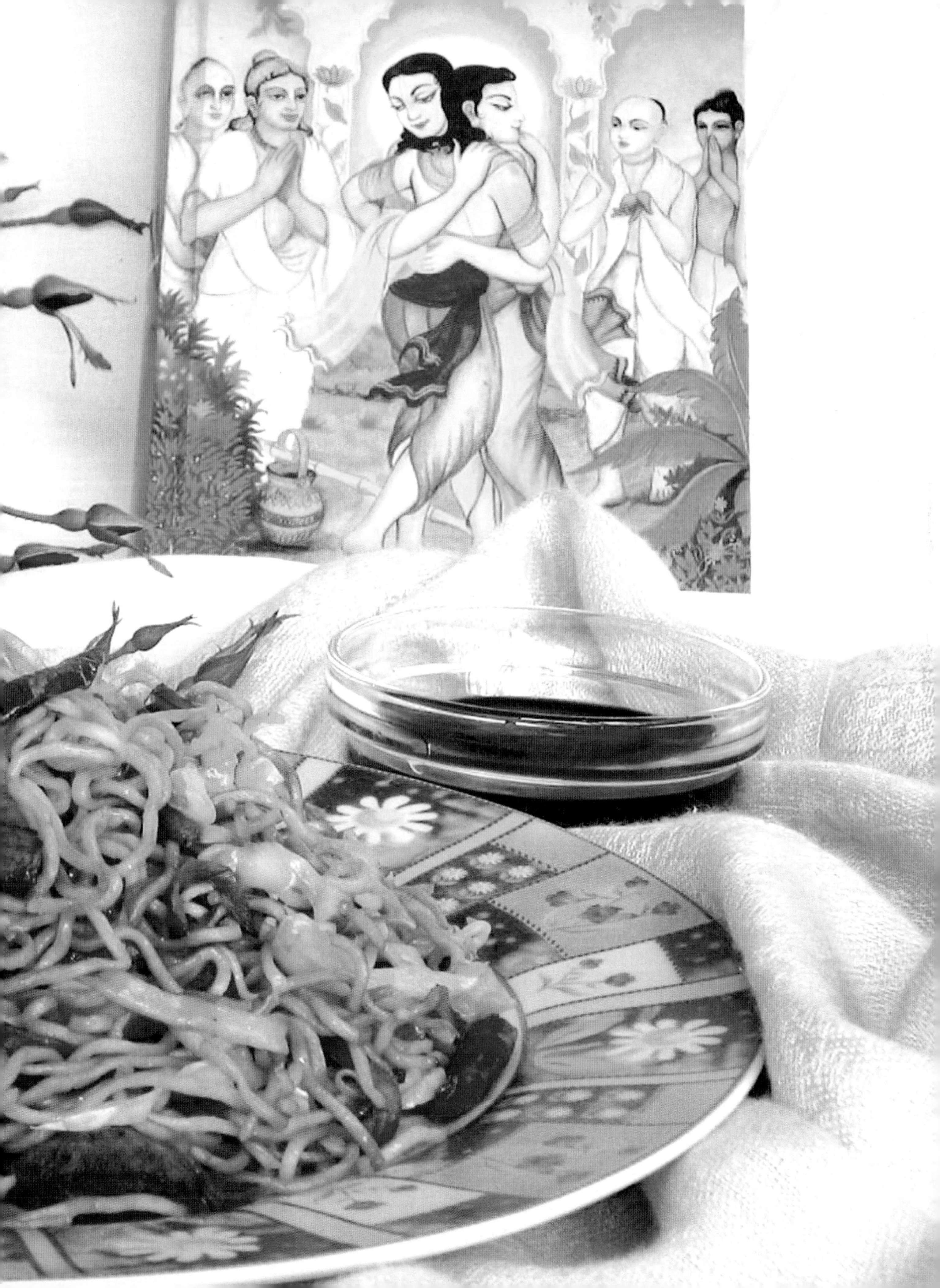

Stir-Fried Noodles

A quick and easy stir-fried Chinese noodles with lots of vegetables.

Preparation time : 30 minutes
Serves : 4 persons

½ cup (125 ml) soya chunks
3 tbs (45 ml) olive oil
6 - 8 curry leaves
½ tsp (2,5 ml) finely grated ginger
½ tsp (2,5 ml) hing
½ cup (125 ml) finely shredded cabbage
2 medium carrots cut into thin strips
A few green beans (50 g) cut into thin diagonal slices
2 medium tomatoes blanched and puréed or use 2 tbs (30 ml) tomato paste
½ cup (125 ml) freshly boiled or frozen green peas
2 tbs (30 ml) soy sauce
1 packet (250 g) instant noodles boiled, then drained
1 tsp (5 ml) salt
1 tbs (15 ml) finely chopped fresh coriander

• Boil the soya chunks until soft. Drain and squeeze out the excess water. Fry until golden brown and crisp.
• Heat the olive oil in a large wok.
• Add the curry leaves, ginger and hing followed by the cabbage, carrots and green beans. Stir-fry until the vegetables are soft yet crisp.
• Add the tomato and cook for a few moments.
• Toss in the peas, soya, noodles, soy sauce and salt.
• Garnish with coriander.

* Variations: Use boiled macaroni in place of noodles. Add an extra ¼ cup (60 ml) corn kernels and some black pepper.

Spaghetti with Italian Tomato Sauce

A tasty spaghetti dish with tomato, olives and Italian herbs. Serve with pesto sauce.

Preparation time : 30 minutes
Serves : 4 persons

3 tbs (45 ml) olive oil
¼ green pepper cut into thin strips
½ cup (125 ml) finely shredded cabbage
1 tsp (5 ml) oregano
1 tsp (5 ml) basil
½ tsp (2,5 ml) hing
¼ cup (60 ml) olive sliced into halves
4 medium tomatoes (approx 460 g) blanched and puréed
1 tsp (5 ml) salt
1 tsp (5 ml) sugar
1 packet (400 g) spaghetti boiled in 2 litres salted water until al-dente, then drained

• Heat the olive oil in a medium-sized heavy-based saucepan.
• Sauté the green pepper and cabbage until soft.
• Add the oregano, basil, hing, olives and tomato.
• Allow to simmer for 15 minutes or until the tomato is well cooked.
• Fold in the salt, sugar and spaghetti.

Pesto sauce

1 cup (250 ml) loosely packed fresh sweet basil
1 cup (250 ml) loosely packed thyme
¼ tsp (1,2 ml) salt
¼ cup (60 ml) pine nuts
1 tbs (15 ml) olive oil
1 tsp (5 ml) lemon juice
¼ tsp (1,2 ml) hing

Remove the coarse stalks from the herbs.
Using a spice grinder, blend all the ingredients into a smooth paste.

Baked Macaroni with Cheese Sauce

This version of baked macaroni and cheese sauce includes fried eggplant rings and has a subtle flavour of nutmeg and cayenne pepper.

Preparation time : 30 minutes
Baking time : 30 minutes
Serves : 4 - 6 persons

Step one: Preparing the macaroni
Boil macaroni (500 g) in lightly salted water until al-dente, then drain. Set asside

Step two: Preparing the cheese sauce
2 tbs (30 ml) butter
4 tbs (60 ml) flour
2 cups (500 ml) milk
1 ½ tsp (7,5 ml) salt
¼ tsp (1,2 ml) black pepper
½ tsp (2,5 ml) cayenne pepper
¼ tsp (1,2 ml) hing
¼ tsp (1,2 ml) nutmeg
½ cup (125 ml) or 50 g grated cheddar cheese

- Melt the butter in a medium-sized heavy-based saucepan.
- Add the flour and braise for a few moments.
- Whisk in the milk, salt, black pepper, cayenne pepper, hing and nutmeg.
- Stir continuously until the sauce thickens.
- Fold in the cheese and macaroni.

Step three: Assembling
1 small eggplant (approx 100 g) cut into thin rounds, sprinkled with ¼ tsp (1,2 ml) salt, then deep-fried until soft yet crisp
½ cup (125 ml) or 50 g grated cheddar cheese
½ tsp (2,5 ml) paprika
1 medium tomato cut into thin rounds
1 tbs (15 ml) finely chopped parsley

- Place half the macaroni and cheese sauce in approx a 15 cm by 20 cm dish that is at least 5 cm deep.
- Spread the fried eggplant evenly on top followed by the remaining macaroni.
- Sprinkle with cheese and paprika.
- Decorate with tomato slices.
- Bake in a preheated moderate oven at 180° C or 350° F for about 30 minutes or until the cheese melts and forms golden brown speckles.
- Garnish with parsley.

* Variations: Omit the eggplant. Serve either plain or use a different vegetable such as zucchini.

Bean and Broccoli Lasagne
Here is a wholesome and delicious dish that contains red kidney beans and broccoli.

Preparation time: 45 minutes
Baking time: 30 minutes
Serves: 4 - 6 persons

Step one: *Preparing the beans and broccoli stew*
2 tbs (30 ml) olive oil
1 tsp (5 ml) fresh thyme
¼ tsp (1,2 ml) hing
1 small broccoli (approx 230 g) cut into medium-sized florets
4 tbs (60 ml) tomato paste
1 can (425 g) red kidney beans
1 cup (250 ml) water
1 tsp (5 ml) salt

- Heat the olive oil in a medium-sized heavy-based saucepan.
- Add the thyme, hing, broccoli and water. Allow to simmer until the vegetable is tender yet crisp.
- Fold in the tomato paste and kidney beans, water and salt. Allow to simmer for a further 5 minutes.

Step two: *Preparing the cheese sauce*
2 tbs (30 ml) butter
2 tbs (30 ml) flour
1 bay leaf
2 cups (500 ml) milk
1 tsp (5 ml) salt
¼ tsp (1,2 ml) black pepper
¼ tsp (1,2 ml) nutmeg

½ cup (125 ml) or 50 g grated cheddar cheese
- Melt the butter in small heavy-based saucepan.
- Add the flour and bay leaf and braise for a few moments.
- Whisk in the milk, salt, black pepper, nutmeg and hing.
- Stirring continuously, simmer until the sauce begins to thicken.
- Fold in the cheese.

Step three: *Assembling*
250 g lasagna sheets (choose ones that do not require precooking)
½ cup (125 ml) or 50 g grated cheddar cheese
Parmesan cheese

- Line a large dish (approx 15 cm by 20 cm) with about half a cup (125 ml) of the bean sauce.
- Layer alternatively with lasagne, beans and broccoli stew and cheese sauce. Use 4 sheets for one layer and end with cheese sauce.
- Sprinkle liberally with cheddar cheese and parmesan cheese.
- Bake in a preheated moderate oven at 180° C or 350° F for about 30 minutes or until the cheese melts and forms golden brown speckles.

Spinach and Cream Cheese Cannelloni

A delightful dish with pasta tubes called cannelloni, filled with cream cheese and spinach, then baked in a cheese sauce. Use cannelloni that does not require precooking.

Preparation time: 30 minutes
Baking time: 30 minutes
Serves: 4 - 6 persons

Step one: Filling the cannelloni tubes

1 bunch of spinach (approx 300 g) finely chopped
1 cup (250 ml) or 200 g cream cheese
½ tsp (2,5 ml) salt
¼ tsp (1,2 ml) black pepper
100 g cannelloni tubes

- Steam the spinach with as little water as possible.
- Drain in a colander but keep the spinach water to add to the cheese sauce.
- Fold the spinach, cream cheese and seasoning together.
- Fill the tubes and place them large dish (about 15 cm by 20 cm).

Step two: Preparing the cheese sauce and assembling

2 tbs (30 ml) butter
2 tbs (30 ml) flour
¼ tsp (1,2 ml) ground nutmeg
¼ tsp (1,2 ml) hing
2 cups (500 ml) milk
½ tsp (2,5 ml) salt
¼ tsp (1,2 ml) black pepper
1 cup (250 ml) or 100 g grated cheese
½ tsp (2,5 ml) paprika
1 tbs (15 ml) finely chopped parsley

- Melt the butter in a medium-sized heavy-based saucepan.
- Stir in the flour, nutmeg and hing. Braise for a few moments.
- Whisk in the milk, salt and pepper. Stir continuously and allow to simmer until the sauce thickens.
- Fold in the spinach water and half the cheese.
- Pour the sauce over the tubes and sprinkle with the remaining cheese and paprika.
- Bake in a preheated moderate oven at 180° C or 350° F for about 30 minutes or until the tubes are well cooked and the cheese melts and forms golden brown speckles.
- Garnish with parsley.

* Variations: Steamed butternut can be used in place of spinach.

Breads and Cereals

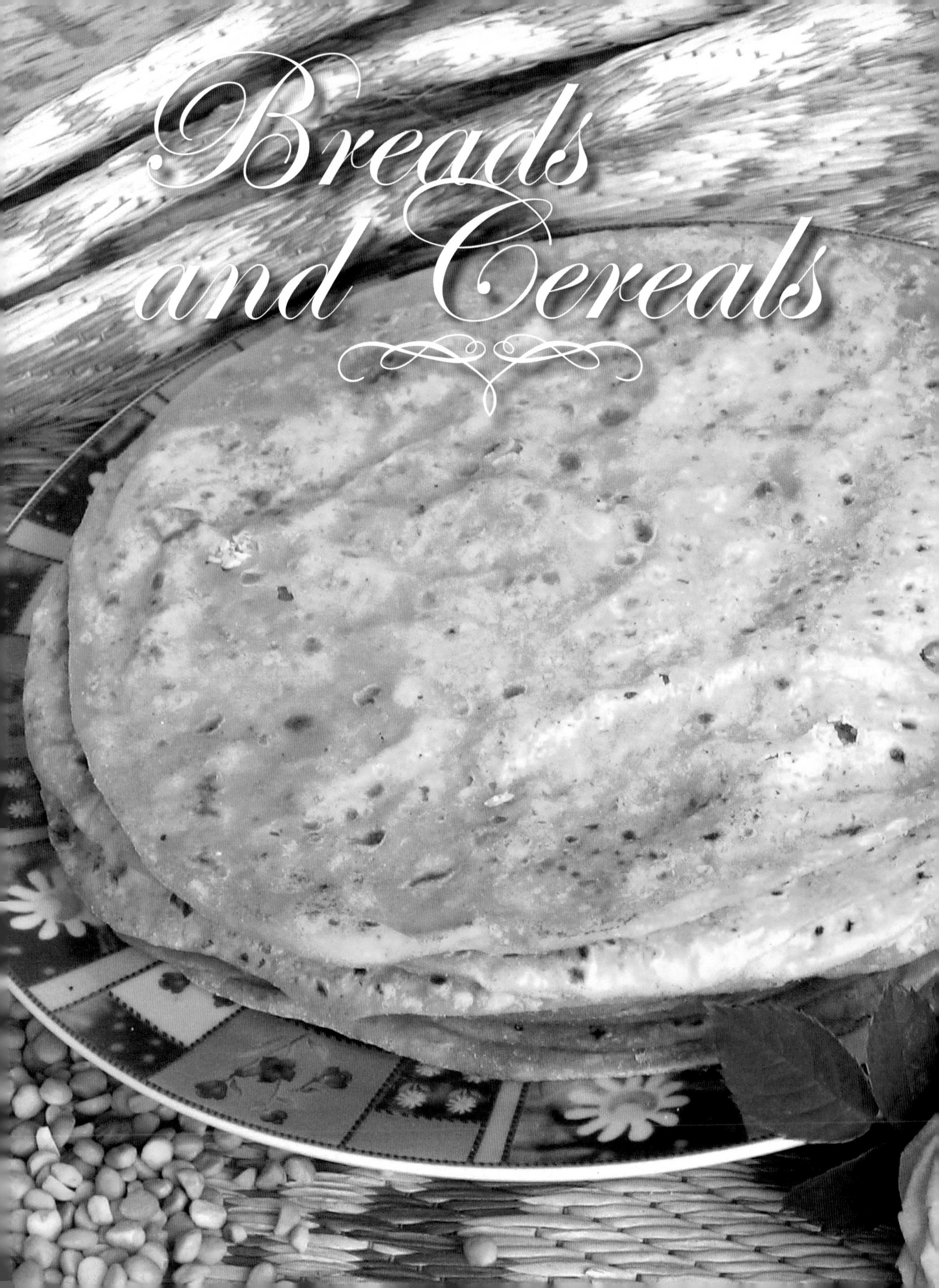

Flat Bread with Dhal Filling (Dhal Roti)

Soft Rolls

These butter soft rolls are perfect for vegetarian burgers or can be formed into smaller elegant dinner rolls. It is not necessary to double rise the dough when using instant yeast, especially if you do not have much preparation time - although I have included this technique as it produces lighter bread. This can apply for all the yeast recipes in this book.

Preparation time: 20 minutes
Rising time: 1 ½ hour
Baking time: 25 - 30 minutes
Makes: 6 large rolls

4 cups (100 ml) flour
1 ½ tsp (7,5 ml) salt
2 tbs (30 ml) instant yeast
1 tsp (5 ml) sugar
4 tbs (60 ml) butter or ghee
Approx 1 ¾ cup (430 ml) luke warm water
Sesame seeds or poppy seeds for sprinkling

- Sift the flour and salt together.
- Mix in the yeast and sugar.
- Rub in the butter or ghee.
- Add enough water to form a soft a pliable dough.
- Knead for 10 minutes.
- Cover and set aside in a warm place to rise for about 1 hour or until double.
- Punch back the dough and form into 6 smooth rolls. Place well apart on a lightly greased baking tray.
- Glaze with milk and sprinkle with seeds.
- Allow to rise again for about 30 minutes.
- Bake in a preheated moderate oven at 180° C or 350° F for about 25 - 30 minutes or until golden brown.

* Variations: Form the dough into a loaf and bake as a bread.
or
Add a ¼ cup (60 ml) sugar, 1 teaspoon (5 ml) mixed spice or cinnamon powder and ¼ cup (60 ml) raisins to the dough for a sweet spicy raisin bun.

Milk glaze for pastries and breads
To create a wonderful rich golden brown colour for pastries and breads, make a paste using 4 tablespoons (60 ml) water and 2 tablespoons (30 ml) milk powder. Glaze before baking.

Croissants

These flaky crescent breads are ideal for breakfast.

Preparation time: 30 minutes
Rising time: 1 hour
Baking time: 25 - 30 minutes
Makes: 6 large breads

- Follow the same dough recipe for soft rolls, only decrease the butter by half. (see page 108)
- Roll out into a large rectangle and dot with cold butter - the same way as you would when making puff pastry. (Photo 1)
- Fold into a neat parcel and place in the fridge for 15 minutes. (Photo 2)

- Roll out again and repeat the process.
- For the third rolling, roll out into a large rectangle and cut out large triangles. Roll up into neat crescents. Glaze with milk and allow to rise for about 30 minutes or until double. (Photo 3)
- Bake as for soft rolls.

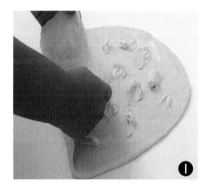

Croissants

Quick Rolls

Here is a quick bread recipe that requires no rising time.

Preparation time: 15 minutes
Baking time: 15 - 20 minutes
Makes: 6 rolls

2 cups (500 ml) flour
½ tsp (2,5 ml) salt
4 tsp (20 ml) baking powder
1 tsp (5 ml) sugar
½ tbs (7,5 ml) butter
Approx ½ cup (125 ml) milk
Milk for glazing
Poppy seeds for sprinkling

• Sift the flour, salt and baking powder together.
• Stir in the sugar and rub in the butter.
• Add enough milk to form a soft dough.
• Form into 6 buns and place on a lightly greased baking tray.
• Glaze with milk and sprinkle with poppy seeds.
• Bake in a preheated moderate oven for at 190° C or 375° F for about 15 - 20 minutes or until golden brown.

Serving suggestion: Serve for a breakfast treat with cheese and tomato or jam.

* Variations: Plait, knot or make into crescents.

Savoury Bread

A spicy bread that has the subtle flavours of the Far East.

Preparation time: 20 minutes
Rising time: 1 ½ hours
Baking time: 45 minutes
Makes: one loaf

3 cups (750 ml) white flour
1 ½ tsp (7,5 ml) salt
½ tsp (2,5 ml) sugar
1 tbs (15 ml) instant yeast
2 tbs (30 ml) oil or ghee
½ tsp (2,5 ml) mustard seeds
½ tsp (2,5 ml) cumin seeds
1 chili finely chopped
6 - 8 curry leaves
2 tbs (30 ml) finely chopped fresh coriander
Approx 1 cup (250 ml) warm water

• Sift the flour and salt together.
• Mix in the sugar and yeast.
• Heat the oil or ghee in a small saucepan.
• Add the mustard seeds and when they begin to splutter, add the cumin seeds, chili and curry leaves.
• Fold the mixture and coriander into the flour. Add enough water to form a soft pliable dough.
• Knead well for 10 minutes and allow to rise in a warm place for about 1 hour or until double.
• Punch back the dough and form into a large oblong shape.
• Place in a greased bread pan and brush with milk. Allow to rise again for about 30 minutes.
• Bake in a preheated moderately hot oven at 190° C or 375° F for about 45 minutes or until golden brown.

Serving suggestion: Serve with hot dhal, potato stir-fry and fresh green salad.

Wholewheat Rolls with Homemade Cheese, Tomato and Olive Filling

Dainty rolls filled with curd flavoured with Italian herbs. Use white or a combination of white and wholewheat flour as an alternative to pure wholewheat flour.

Preparation time: 30 minutes
Rising time: 1 ½ hour
Baking time: 25 - 30 minutes
Makes: 8 rolls

Step one: Preparing the dough

2 cups (500 ml) wholewheat flour
1 tsp (5 ml) salt
1 tbs (15 ml) instant yeast
½ tsp (2,5 ml) sugar
2 tbs (30 ml) butter, oil or ghee
Approx ½ cup (125 ml) warm water
Milk for glazing
½ tbs (7,5 ml) sesame seeds for sprinkling

- Sift the flour and salt together.
- Mix in the yeast and sugar.
- Rub in the butter, oil or ghee.
- Add enough water to form a soft pliable dough.
- Knead well for 10 minutes.
- Cover and set aside in a warm place to rise for about 1 hour or until double.
- In the meantime prepare the filling.

Step two: Preparing the filling

¾ cup (180 ml) or 115 g curd made from 1 litre full cream milk
1 medium tomato finely diced
½ tsp (2,5 ml) basil
½ tsp (2,5 ml) oregano
¼ tsp (1,2 ml) hing
2 tbs (30 ml) sliced olives
½ tsp (2,5 ml) salt
2 tbs (30 ml) olive oil

Crumble the curd and fold in the rest of the ingredients.

Step three: Assembling

- Punch back the dough and divide into 8 balls.
- Press into hat-like discs and place about one tablespoon (15 ml) filling in each. Pinch closed.
- Gently mould into oval shapes.
- Using a knife, scar each with 3 diagonal lines.
- Glaze with milk, sprinkle with sesame seeds and allow to rise again for about 30 minutes.
- Bake in a preheated moderate oven at 180° C or 350° F for about 25 - 30 minutes or until golden brown.

Serving suggestion: Serve as a meal on its own or as a side dish.

* Variations: In place of the olives and Italian herbs, add ¼ cup (60 ml) green peas, ¼ cup (60 ml) corn kernels and basic oriental spicing.

Pita Bread

Cook this famous Middle Eastern flat bread on a griddle pan or bake in a hot oven.

Preparation time: 30 minutes
Rising time: 1 ½ hour
Makes: 8 breads

1 cup (250 ml) wholewheat flour
1 cup (250 ml) white flour
1 tsp (5 ml) salt
1 tbs (15 ml) instant yeast
½ tsp (2,5 ml) sugar
1 tbs (15 ml) butter or ghee
Approx ¾ cup (180 ml) water

• Sift the flours and salt together.
• Mix in the yeast and sugar.
• Rub in the butter or ghee.
• Add enough water to form a soft pliable dough.
• Knead well for 10 minutes.
• Cover and set aside in a warm place to rise for about 1 hour or until double.

• Punch back the dough and divide into 8 balls
• Dredge each ball with flour and roll out into about 10 cm rounds.
• Place well apart on a lightly floured surface and allow to rise for about 30 minutes or until double.
• Place a round on a hot griddle pan. As the bread balloons and forms light brown speckles, turn over to cook on the other side.
• Repeat the process until all the breads are cooked.
• Wrap in a cloth to keep warm.

Serving suggestion: Fill the pockets with salad or curry.

Corn Bread

A delicious farm style corn baked bread.

Preparation time: 15 minutes
Baking time: 1 hour
Makes: one loaf

1 cup (250 ml) flour
½ tsp (2,5 ml) salt
2 tsp (10 ml) baking powder
2 cups (500 ml) finely minced, ready cooked yellow corn kernels
¼ cup (60 ml) butter
¾ cup (180 ml) sugar
2 tbs (30 ml) yoghurt
2 tbs (30 ml) coconut
1 tsp (5 ml) vanilla essence

• Sift the flour, salt and baking powder together.
• Cream the corn, butter, sugar, yoghurt, coconut and vanilla essence together.
• Fold the creamed mixture into the flour.
• Place into a greased loaf pan and bake in a preheated moderate oven at 180° C or 350° F for about 1 hour or until the bread is well cooked and golden brown.

Serving suggestion: Great for breakfast, serve with butter and fig jam or cheese.

Tomato Scones with Cream Cheese Filling

A feather light savoury scone that can be served with tea.

Preparation time: 30 minutes
Baking time: 20 - 25 minutes
Makes: 6 scones

Step one: Preparing the scones

1¾ cup (430 ml) flour
2 tsp (10 ml) baking powder
½ tsp (2,5 ml) salt
¼ tsp (1,2 ml) hing
¼ tsp (1,2 ml) sugar
2 tbs (30 ml) butter
½ medium tomato finely diced
1 tbs (15 ml) lemon juice
Approx ¾ cup (180 ml) milk

- Sift the flour, baking powder, salt and hing together.
- Stir in the sugar and rub in the butter.
- Fold in the tomato and lemon juice.
- Add enough milk to form a soft dough.
- Roll out on a lightly floured surface into about a 2 cm thick rectangle.
- Use a scone cutter or the rim of a glass dipped in flour and cut out rounds.
- Place well apart on to a lightly greased baking tray and glaze with milk.
- Bake in a preheated moderate oven at 190° C or 375° F for about 20 - 25 minutes or until golden brown.

Step two: Preparing the filling

115 g curd made from 1 litre full cream milk or ¾ cup (180 ml) cream cheese
½ medium tomato finely diced
½ tsp (2,5 ml) salt
¼ tsp (1,2ml) black pepper
1 tbs (15 ml) olive oil
1 tbs (15 ml) finely chopped parsley

- Crumble the curd or using the cream cheese, fold all the ingredients together.
- Halve the scones and sandwich with a generous amount of filling.

Pizza

Italian pizzas are fun to make. Here is an easy recipe for you to follow that will give a light medium thick base. If you like your pizzas thinner simply roll out the dough into larger rounds.

Preparation time: 30 minutes
Rising time: 1 ½ hour
Baking time: 25 minutes
Makes: one large pizza

Step one: Preparing the base

1 ½ cups (375 ml) flour
¾ tsp (5 ml) salt
½ tsp (2,5 ml) sugar
½ tsp (2,5 ml) oregano
1 tbs (15 ml) instant yeast
1 tbs (15 ml) oil or ghee
Approx ¾ cup (180 ml) warm water

- Sift the flour and salt together.
- Mix in the sugar, oregano, yeast and oil or ghee.
- Gradually add the water until a soft pliable dough forms.
- Knead well for 10 minutes. Allow to rise in a warm place for about 1 hour or until double.
- Punch back and roll out into about a 23 cm round. Place on a lightly greased baking tray and allow to rise again for about 30 minutes.
- Blind bake in a preheated moderate oven 180° C or 350° F for 10 minutes.

Step two: Preparing the tomato chutney

1 tbs (15 ml) olive oil
½ cup (125 ml) finely shredded cabbage
2 medium tomatoes blanched and puréed
¼ tsp (1,2 ml) oregano
¼ tsp (1,2 ml) basil
¼ tsp (1,2 ml) hing
¼ tsp (1,2 ml) salt

- Heat the olive oil in a small heavy-based saucepan.
- Braise the cabbage and add the rest of the ingredients.
- Allow to simmer for 10 minutes or until the tomato is well cooked.

Step three: Assembling

- Spread the tomato chutney on the base of the pizza.
- Sprinkle with mozzarella cheese.
- Top with artichokes, grated bell pepper, olives and a few slivers of fried eggplant or as desired.
- Place back in the oven for about 15 minutes or until the cheese melts and forms golden brown speckles.

Granola

A crunchy cereal mix rich in protein and enzymes.

Preparation time: 15 minutes
Baking time: 1 hour
Makes: 690 g cereal

½ cup (125 ml) butter
½ cup (125 ml) golden syrup
5 ¾ cups (1430 ml) or 500 g oats
¼ cup (60 ml) cashew nuts
¼ cup (60 ml) almond nuts
2 tbs (30 ml) sesame seeds
2 tbs (30 ml) sunflower seeds
¼ cup (60 ml) coconut slivers (optional)
½ cup (125 ml) raisins
Mixed dried fruits

- Melt the butter over low heat and stir in the golden syrup. Turn off the heat.
- Fold in the oat, nuts, seeds and coconut until well coated.
- Spread in a large tray and bake in a preheated moderate oven at 180° C or 350° F for about 1 hour or until a rich golden brown colour. Stir at 10 minute intervals to prevent burning.
- Fold in the raisins and dried fruits
- Store in an airtight container.

Banana and Raisin Muffins

Eggless wholewheat fruit muffins are delicious for breakfast.

Preparation time: 15 minutes
Baking time: 25 minutes
Makes: 6 muffins

2 cups (500 ml) wholewheat flour
3 tsp (15 ml) baking powder
½ cup (125 ml) butter
⅓ cup (80 ml) sugar
2 tsp (10 ml) vanilla essence
2 mashed bananas
¼ cup (60 ml) raisins
Approx ¾ cup (180 ml) milk

- Sift the flour and baking powder together.
- Cream the butter, sugar, vanilla essence and bananas.
- Add the raisins.
- Fold all the ingredients together gradually adding the milk until a thick batter forms. (Do not over mix.)
- Grease a muffin tray and divide the batter between six compartments.
- Bake in a preheated moderate oven at 180° C or 350° F for about 25 minutes or until the muffins are golden brown.
- Allow to cool before removing from the tray.

Fried Puffed Wholewheat Bread (Poori)

Popular Indian flat breads that puff up into balloon shapes as they are being fried. Although this recipe features pure wholewheat flour, you can make pooris using different combinations of flours for example, ½ wholewheat and ½ white flour.

Preparation time: 30 minutes
Resting time: ½ - 3 hours
Makes: 12 breads

1 ½ cups (375 ml) pure wholewheat flour
½ tsp (2,5 ml) salt
1 tbs (15 ml) butter or ghee
Approx ¾ cup (180 ml) water

- Sift the flour and salt together.
- Rub in the butter or ghee and gradually add the water to form a soft pliable dough.
- Knead for 10 minutes.
- Cover and set aside to rest for ½ - 3 hours.
- Knead again and divide the dough into 12 balls.
- Dredge each ball with flour and roll out into about 12 cm rounds.

- Deep-fry in small batches (2 or 3 at a time) in moderate hot oil.
- Turn over as the pooris begin to puff.
- Once fully ballooned, slightly crisp and light golden brown in colour remove from the oil and drain.

Serving suggestion: These breads are best served hot to accompany an oriental meal. They can also be sandwiched together with desired fillings.

* Variations: Add 2 tablespoons (30 ml) sesame seed to the dough.

Non-Grain Fried Puffed Bread (Non-grain Poori)

For people suffering from wheat allergies this bread can be a great substitute for wholewheat pooris.

Preparation time: 20 minutes
Makes: 10 small pooris

1 cup (250 ml) full cream milk powder
½ cup (125 ml) starch, potato or tapioca flour
½ tsp (2,5 ml) salt
1 tsp (5 ml) butter or ghee
Approx ¼ cup (60 ml) water

- Sift the milk powder, starch, potato or tapioca flour and salt together.
- Rub in the butter or ghee.
- Add just enough water to form a soft pliable dough. Knead well.
- Lightly sprinkle a large surface with starch powder and roll out into about a 0,5 cm deep rectangle.

- Dip the rim of a glass or scone cutter in starch and cut out rounds.
- Deep-fry the pooris in small batches in fairly low heated oil until golden brown on both sides, then drain.

Hint: Add the water cautiously so that the dough is of the right constituency. If the dough becomes too dry, knead in a few more drops of water.

Serving suggestions: A light potato curry and peanut and mint chutney are good accompaniments for pooris.

Grilled Wholewheat Bread (Chapati)

*These are traditional Indian flat breads that are made with pure wholewheat flour.
Atta flour is best but not always readily available in the West. The breads are cooked
on a griddle pan and then placed over an open flame where they puff up into
balloon shapes.*

Preparation time: 30 minutes
Rising time: 3 hours
Makes: 10 breads

2 cups (500 ml) pure wholewheat flour
½ tsp (2,5 ml) salt
Approx ¾ cup (180 ml) water

- Sift the flour and salt together.
- Add enough water to form a soft pliable dough.
- Knead well for 10 minutes.
- Cover and allow to rest for at least 3 hours.
- Knead once more and divide into 10 balls.
- Dredge each ball with flour and roll out into
  about 15 cm rounds. (Photo 1)
- Gently place one of the rounds on a preheated
  griddle pan and allow to cook until the underside
  shows brown speckles.
- Turn over and cook on the other side. (Photo 2)
- Lift the chapati with a tong and place
  over an open flame, turning gently as it
  balloons. (Photo 3)
- Remove from the flame and dab with butter.
- Repeat the process until all the chapatis are cooked.
  Stack on top of one another and keep covered
  with a dry cloth so that they remain warm.

Serving suggestion: Best served hot, these griddle
breads can accompany almost any meal. Different
fillings can be rolled up in these healthy breads
making them great for the lunch box. Try chickpeas
and tomato curry or potato chutney.
or
For a quick filling simply grate some cheese,
add some tomato wedges and shredded lettuce.

BREAD AND CEREALS

Griddled Flat Indian Bread (Roti)

A flat bread resembling a pancake that is cooked on a griddle pan or large frying pan.
White flour, wholewheat flour or a combination of both these flours can be used.

Preparation time : 30 minutes
Makes : 10 large rotis

1 ½ cup (375 ml) wholewheat flour
1 ½ cup (375 ml) white flour
1 tsp (5 ml) salt
¼ cup (60 ml) oil, butter or ghee
Approx 1 cup (250 ml) boiling hot water

- Sift the flours and salt together.
- Rub in the oil, butter or ghee.
- Gradually add the boiling water until a soft pliable dough forms. (Use a wooden spoon for this purpose and be careful not to add too much water, as the flour will absorb the water very easily.)
- Knead well and keep covered until ready to use.

- Divide the dough into 10 balls and roll out on a lightly floured surface into about 20 cm rounds.
- Place a roti on a hot griddle pan. When lightly speckled brown underneath, flip over and cook on the other side.
- Rub with melted butter as the roti cooks.
- Repeat the process until all the rotis are cooked.
- While cooking, stack on top of one another and keep covered with a cloth so that they remain warm.

Serving suggestion : Rotis can be served with a vegetable or a bean curry.

Flat Bread with Dhal Filling (Dhal Roti)

These breads are very famous in Mauritius. Almost every housewife knows how to prepare them.

Preparation time : 45 minutes
Makes : 10 rotis

Step one: Preparing the dough
2 cups (500 ml) flour
½ tsp (2,5 ml) salt
1 tbs (15 ml) oil or ghee
Approx ¾ cup (180 ml) boiling water

- Sift the flour and salt together.
- Rub in the oil or ghee.
- Gradually add enough boiling water to form a soft pliable dough.
- Cover and set aside until the filling is ready.

Step two: Preparing the filling
¾ cups (180 ml) or 100 g yellow gram dhal
½ tsp (2,5 ml) salt
1 tsp (5 ml) finely ground cumin seeds

- Boil the dhal for about 10 minutes or until it is soft enough to crush between the fingers.

- Drain and grind into a fine powder. A food processor can be used for this purpose. (Do not add water.)
- Mix in the salt and cumin.

Step three: Assembling and cooking
- Divide the dough into 10 balls.
- Pat into hat-like discs and fill each with about 2 tablespoons (30 ml) of filling, then pinch the tops closed.
- Dip in flour and roll out into about 12 cm rounds.
- Place one round on a heated griddle pan.
- When speckles of brown appear underneath turn over and cook on the other side. Rub both sides with butter as the roti cooks.
- Cook all the same way. Stack one on top of another and keep wrapped in a large cloth to keep warm.

Serving suggestion : Serve the same way as for rotis.

Layered Griddled Bread (Paratha)

These breads are very similar to rotis, the only difference being that they are flakier and richer as they require more shortening while folding. The rolling can be done in different ways. Here I have suggested two popular techniques.

Preparation time: 30 - 40 minutes
Makes: 10 breads

Method one
- Make dough as for rotis *(see page 118)*. Divide into 10 parts and roll out into about 20 cm rounds.
- Spread 1 teaspoon (5 ml) oil on each round and folded up into neat little squares as if you are making puff pastry.
- Roll out into about 18 cm squares and cook as for rotis. The paratha will puff up like a balloon as the trapped air expands while heating, forming its flaky character.

Method two
- Make dough as for rotis *(see page 118)*. Divide into 10 parts and roll out into about 20 cm rounds.
- Spread 1 teaspoon (5 ml) oil on the surface of each roti.
- Make a slit from the centre to the edge and roll up into a spiral. Press into a neat bun, dredge with flour and roll out into about 18 cm rounds.
- Cook on a griddle pan as for rotis.

Stuffed Griddled Bread (Stuffed Paratha)

Roti dough forms the basis of this bread. A variety of fillings can be made. Try any one of the suggested fillings below.

Preparation time: 45 minutes
Makes: 10 breads

Assembling and cooking the paratha
- Make dough as for rotis *(see page 118)*. Divide into 10 parts and roll out into about 18 cm rounds.
- Divide the filling into 10 parts. Spread evenly on half of each roti.
- Fold over and seal with a fork.
- Cook on a griddle pan until light speckles of brown appear on both sides.
- Rub with melted butter as the paratha cooks.

Filling one: Braised cabbage
2 cups (500 ml) finely grated cabbage.
1 tbs (15 ml) oil or ghee
¼ tsp (1,2 ml) mustard seeds
1 tsp (5 ml) finely grated ginger
½ tsp (2,5 ml) hing
½ tsp (2,5 ml) salt
1 tbs (15 ml) finely chopped fresh coriander

- Heat the oil or ghee in a medium-sized heavy-based saucepan.
- Add the mustard seeds and when they begin to splutter, add the ginger and hing.
- Fold in the cabbage and salt. Braise for a few minutes.
- Fold in the coriander and allow to cool.

Filling two: Sautéed watercress
1 medium-sized bunch of watercress (approx 190 g) finely chopped
1 tbs (15 ml) oil or ghee
1 tsp (5 ml) finely grated ginger
½ tsp (2,5 ml) hing
½ tsp (2,5 ml) salt

- Heat the oil or ghee in a medium-sized heavy-based saucepan.
- Add the ginger and hing.
- Fold in the watercress and salt. Sauté for a few minutes.
- Allow to cool.

Filling three: Cheese and tomato
Grated cheese and some tomato slices, seasoned with salt and pepper.

Desserts and Puddings

Trifle

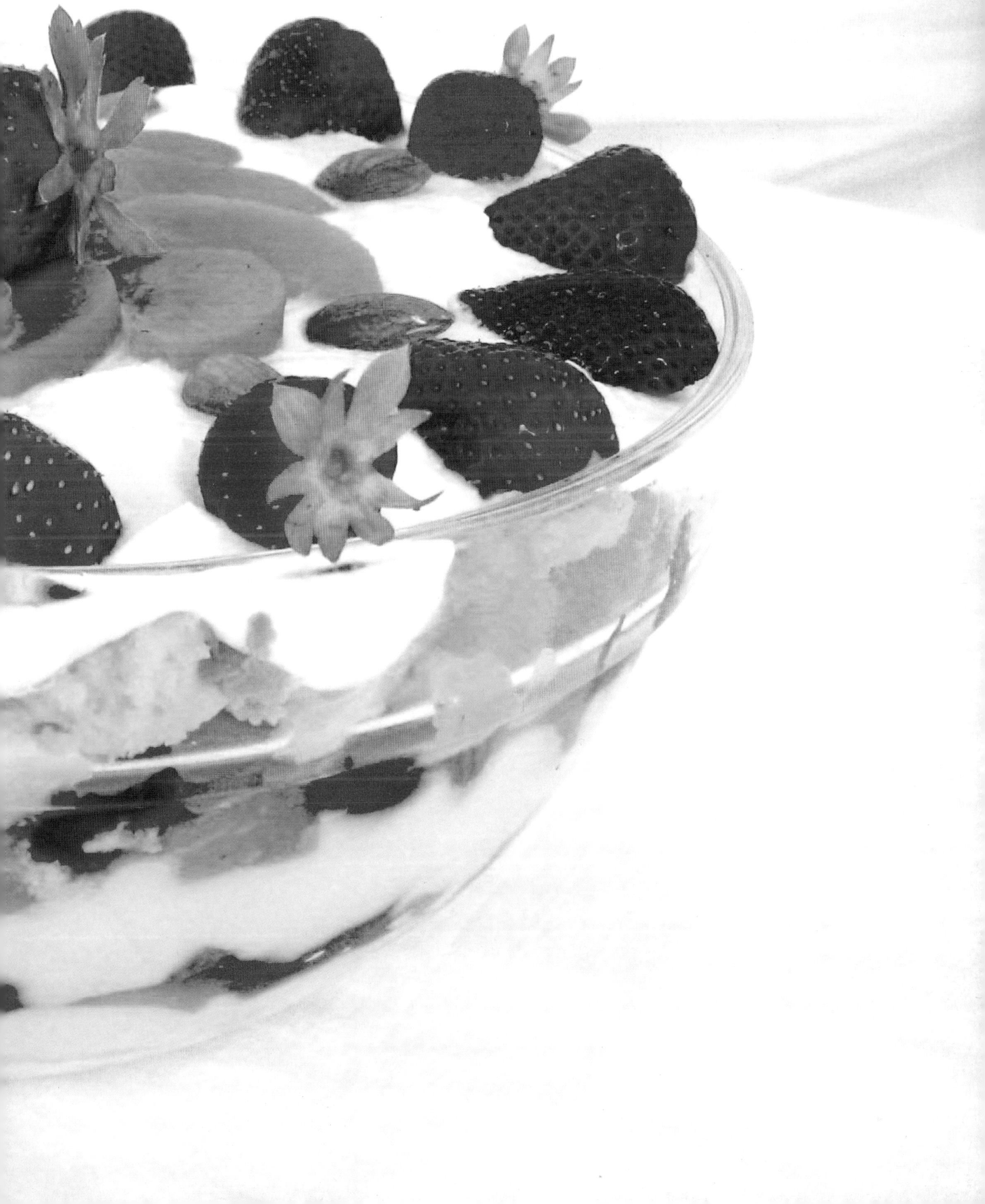

Trifle

To end a special dinner, impress your friends with this grand dessert.

Preparation time : 45 minutes
Serves : 6 - 8 persons

Prepare each of the following items separately before assembling the trifle.

1 small sponge cake [uses ½ the recipe on page 150]
2 cups (500 ml) homemade custard
1 cup (250 ml) vegetarian jelly
½ cup (125 ml) slivered almonds lightly toasted
1 can peach slices and the syrup
1 cup (250 ml) freshly whipped cream
Cherries or strawberries for decorating

Preparing the custard

2 cups (500 ml) milk
4 tbs (60 ml) sugar
1 tbs (15 ml) butter
1 tsp (5 ml) vanilla essence
Pinch of yellow food colour
4 tbs (60 ml) cornflour

• Bring 1 ½ cups of the milk to boil and allow to simmer over low heat.
• Stir in the sugar, butter, vanilla essence and food colour.
• Make a paste with the cornflour and the remaining milk. Add to the simmering milk.
• Stir until thick, then set aside.

Preparing the vegetarian jelly

1 cup (250 ml) water
1 tbs (15 ml) sugar
1 tsp (5 ml) vanilla essence
1 tsp (5 ml) agar- agar (china grass)
Pinch of red colour

Boil all the ingredients together. Place in fridge for about 15 minutes until firm, then coarsely grate.

Preparing the fresh cream

1 cup (250 ml) fresh cream
1 tbs (15 ml) sugar
1 tsp (5 ml) vanilla essence

Whisk the cream to a soft peak stage. Fold in the sugar and vanilla essence.

Assembling the trifle

• Cut the cake into thin slices and divide into 3 parts.
• Line the bottom of a large dessert bowl with 1 part of the cake and saturate with about 4 tablespoons (60 ml) of the peach syrup. Pour half of the custard over the cake followed by ½ of the peaches, then ½ the jelly and ½ of the nuts.
• Repeat the layer once more ending with the remaining cake and syrup.
• Top with the fresh cream and decorate with cherries or strawberries.
• Place in the fridge for a few hours before serving.

Fruit and Nut Semolina Pudding (Halava)

A roasted semolina dessert with mixed fruit, nuts and orange zest.

Preparation time: 30 minutes
Serves: 4 - 6 persons

3 cups (750 ml) water
1 ¼ cup (310 ml) sugar
1 apple diced into small cubes
¼ pineapple or ½ cup (125 ml) peeled and diced into small cubes
2 bananas peeled and sliced into small rounds
1 cinnamon stick (approx 5 cm)
¼ cup (60 ml) butter
1½ cup (375 ml) semolina
¼ cup (60 ml) almonds or cashew nuts
Zest and juice of ½ orange

• Boil water and sugar together.
• Add the apple, pineapple and the cinnamon stick. Simmer over low heat with the lid on.
• In the meantime melt the butter in a large heavy-based saucepan. Add the semolina and nuts. Braise until light brown.

• Add the bananas to the syrup.
• Add the syrup with the fruit to the semolina. [The mixture will begin to bubble.]
• Keep stirring until the mixture begins to pull away from the sides.
• Fold in the zest and juice of the orange then turn off the heat.

Serving suggestions: Serve as a dessert in individual bowls or place the hot semolina in an ungreased cake tin. Allow to cool. Turn over and serve as a cake garnished with 1 tablespoon (15 ml) coconut.

* Variations: Replace the fruit and nuts with ½ cup (125 ml) of dates without seeds.

Sweet Rice with Orange Zest

This is a popular Bengali dessert made with sweet condensed milk and rice that is of semi-liquid constituency.

Preparation time: 1 hour 15 minutes
Serves: 4 - 6 persons

8 cups (2000 ml) full cream milk
4 cloves
4 opened cardamom pods
1 cinnamon stick (approx 5 cm)
¼ cup (60 ml) basmati rice
¾ cup (180 ml) sugar
Zest from a medium orange

• Bring the milk and spices to a gentle boil, then stir in the rice.
• Continue boiling for at least 1 hour or until the mixture has reduced to half its original volume. Stir occasionally to prevent scorching.
• Mix in the sugar towards the end of the cooking.

• Fold in the orange zest and allow to cool before serving.

* Variations: For other flavours add berries and vanilla essence towards the end of the cooking.
or
Add saffron threads, a pinch of camphor and a few cardamom pods.

La Crème

A delicate milk pudding using agar-agar, a seaweed extract, as its gelling agent in place of gelatine.

Preparation time: 10 - 15 minutes
Setting time: 1 hour
Serves: 4 - 6 persons

4 cups (1000 ml) full cream milk
¼ cup (60 ml) full cream milk powder
¾ cup (180 ml) sugar
2 tsp (10 ml) vanilla essence
1 tbs [15 ml] or 5 g agar - agar (china grass)

• Whisk all ingredients together.
• Bring to a gentle boil in a heavy-based saucepan. Stir continuously to prevent scorching.
• Pour into mould (approx 5 cm deep and 15 cm diameter) and set in the fridge for at least one hour until firm.

• Loosen the sides and turn over onto a plate.

Serving suggestions: Drain the juice from a small can of mixed fruit and spread the fruit on top of the turned over pudding.
or
Set in individual cups instead of a mould and decorate with slightly sweetened freshly whipped cream, grated carob and cherries.

La Crème

Cheese Balls in Cream Sauce (Ras Malai)

One of India's most famous desserts is curd cheese balls cooked in rose syrup and served in lush cream sauce.

Preparation time: 30 minutes
For the sauce: 40 minutes
Makes: 16 balls

Knead 230 g of curd made from 2 litres full cream milk until absolutely smooth.
Roll into 16 smooth crack-free balls.

For the syrup

3 cups (750 ml) sugar
4 cups (1000 ml) water
1 tsp (5 ml) rose essence

- Bring the sugar and water to a gentle boil, then add the cheese balls.
- Cover and allow to gently boil for about 12 minutes or until double in size.
- Stir in the rose essence.
- Allow to the balls to soak for at least an hour before removing the balls from the syrup and folding them into the sauce.

For the sauce

8 cups (2000 ml) full cream milk
4 opened cardamom pods
¾ cup (180 ml) sugar
1 tsp (5 ml) saffron threads infused in 2 tbs (30 ml) milk or water

- Bring the milk and cardamom to a gentle boil. Keep boiling for about 30 minutes or until half its original volume.
- Towards the end of the cooking stir in the sugar and saffron threads.

Serving suggestion: Garnish with coarsely ground pistachio nuts.

Vermicilli Pudding

These thin noodle-like strands make a wonderful sweet pudding.

Preparation time: 20 minutes
Setting time: 1 hour
Makes: 12 pieces

4 cups (1000 ml) milk
3 cups (750 ml) vermicelli slightly crushed
¾ cup (180 ml) sugar
1 tbs (15 ml) butter
Pinch of yellow food colour
1 tsp (5 ml) vanilla essence
4 tbs (60 ml) cornflour
1 tbs (15 ml) coconut for sprinkling

- Bring 3 ½ cups of the milk to boil in a medium-sized heavy-based saucepan and allow to simmer.
- Add the vermicelli, sugar, butter, food colour and vanilla essence. Cook until the vermicelli noodles become soft and translucent.

- Make a paste with the cornflour and the remaining milk. Mix into the vermicelli.
- Keep stirring until the mixture thickens and begins to pull away from the sides.
- Turn off the heat and pour into an approx 18 cm by 25 cm baking tray.
- Sprinkle with coconut.
- Place in the fridge and allow to set for at least 1 hour before cutting into squares.

* Variations: Add ¼ cup (60 ml) raisins while cooking.

DESSERT AND PUDDINGS

Maize Pudding

Maize meal is generally made into porridge for breakfast but here I have turned this dish into a lovely fluffy cake that can be served for dessert.

Preparation time: 20 minutes
Setting time: at least 1 hour
Makes: 1 small pudding for 5 - 6 persons

4 cups (1000 ml) milk
1 cup (250 ml) maize meal
¾ cup (180 ml) sugar
1 tbs (15 ml) butter
¼ cup (60 ml) raisins
1 tbs (15 ml) vanilla essence
Coconut for sprinkling

- Bring the milk to a gentle boil and allow to simmer.
- Add the maize meal, sugar, butter, raisins and vanilla essence.
- Stir continuously until the mixture thickens and begins to pull away from the sides.
- Spoon and flatten into a lightly buttered pudding bowl that is about 5 cm deep.
- Place in the refrigerator for at least one hour to set.
- Turn over onto an attractive plate. Sprinkle with coconut.

Ice – Cream

A deliciously rich ice-cream that can be made with flavours of your choice.

Preparation time: 15 minutes
Freezing time: at least 6 hours
Serves: 4 - 6 persons

3 cups (750 ml) semi-whipped fresh cream
1 can condensed milk (397 g)

Choose any of the following flavours
1 tsp (5 ml) saffron infused in 1 tbs (15 ml) milk or water
2 tbs (30 ml) pistachio nuts coarsely ground
½ tsp (2,5 ml) rose essence
or
¼ cup (60 ml) carob powder dissolved in 2 tbs (30 ml) hot water
¼ cup (60 ml) small carob chunks

2 tsp (10 ml) vanilla essence
or
1 cup (250 ml) mango or strawberry partly crushed
2 tsp (10 ml) vanilla essence

Gently fold any of the chosen flavours and the condensed milk into the cream. Freeze until firm.

Ice - Cream Cake with Peppermint Carob Filling

Impress your friends with this special layered ice-cream cake. Try the suggested fillings for exciting variations.

Preparation time: 15 minutes
Freezing time: 4 ½ hours
Makes: 1 small cake for 5 - 6 persons

1 small vanilla cake
1 cup (250 ml) fruit juice
1 tub ice cream (2 litres)
Peppermint carob bars

- Line a large pudding bowl with aluminium foil.
- Slice the cake into thin triangles and line the bowl (including the sides) with ¾ of the triangles.
- Saturate with some of the juice.
- Place a layer of half the ice-cream on top of the cake. Freeze for 30 minutes or until firm.
- Crumble the peppermint carob bars on top of the layer of ice-cream and freeze for another 30 minutes or until firm.
- Place the remaining ice-cream on top of the carob and freeze for another 30 minutes or until firm.
- Place the remaining cake on top of the ice-cream and saturate with the remaining fruit juice.
- Cover with tin foil and freeze for at least 3 hours before turning over onto an attractive plate.

* Variations: For children's party, use jelly tots or any other colourful sweets for the centre of the cake.
or
For a more formal dinner, try this delicious cheesecake filling. Blend together 175 g cream cheese, ¼ cup (60 ml) lemon juice, 1 tsp (5 ml) vanilla essence and ⅓ cup (80 ml) sweet condensed milk. Fold in some berries. Remember to freeze until firm before adding the next layer of ice-cream.
or
Use different flavours and colours of ice-cream to complement your choice of filling.

DESSERT AND PUDDINGS

Pancakes and Custard

Eggless pancakes with homemade custard make a marvellous dessert.

Preparation time: 30 minutes
Makes: approx 10 pancakes

Step one: Preparing the pancakes

1 cup (250 ml) flour
¼ tsp (1,2 ml) bicarbonate of soda
2 tbs (30 ml) sugar
Approx 1 cup (250 ml) milk

- Sift the flour and bicarbonate together.
- Stir in the sugar and add enough milk to form a pouring batter.
- Melt a blob of butter in a medium-sized heavy-based frying pan and pour in about 3 tablespoons (45 ml) of batter.
- With the back of a tablespoon spread evenly into a large round.
- Once the underneath is speckled brown, loosen the sides and turn over to cook on the other side.
- Repeat the process until all the batter is used.

Step two: Preparing the custard

1 cup (250 ml) milk
1 tbs (15 ml) butter
Pinch of yellow food colour
2 tbs (30 ml) sugar
2 tbs (30 ml) cornflour
1 tsp (5 ml) vanilla essence

- Bring ¾ cup (180 ml) of the milk to a gentle boil and allow to simmer.
- Add the butter, food colour, sugar and vanilla essence.
- Make a paste with the cornflour and remaining milk. Add to the simmering milk.
- Keep stirring until the mixture thickens.

Place a generous amount of custard in each pancake and roll up.

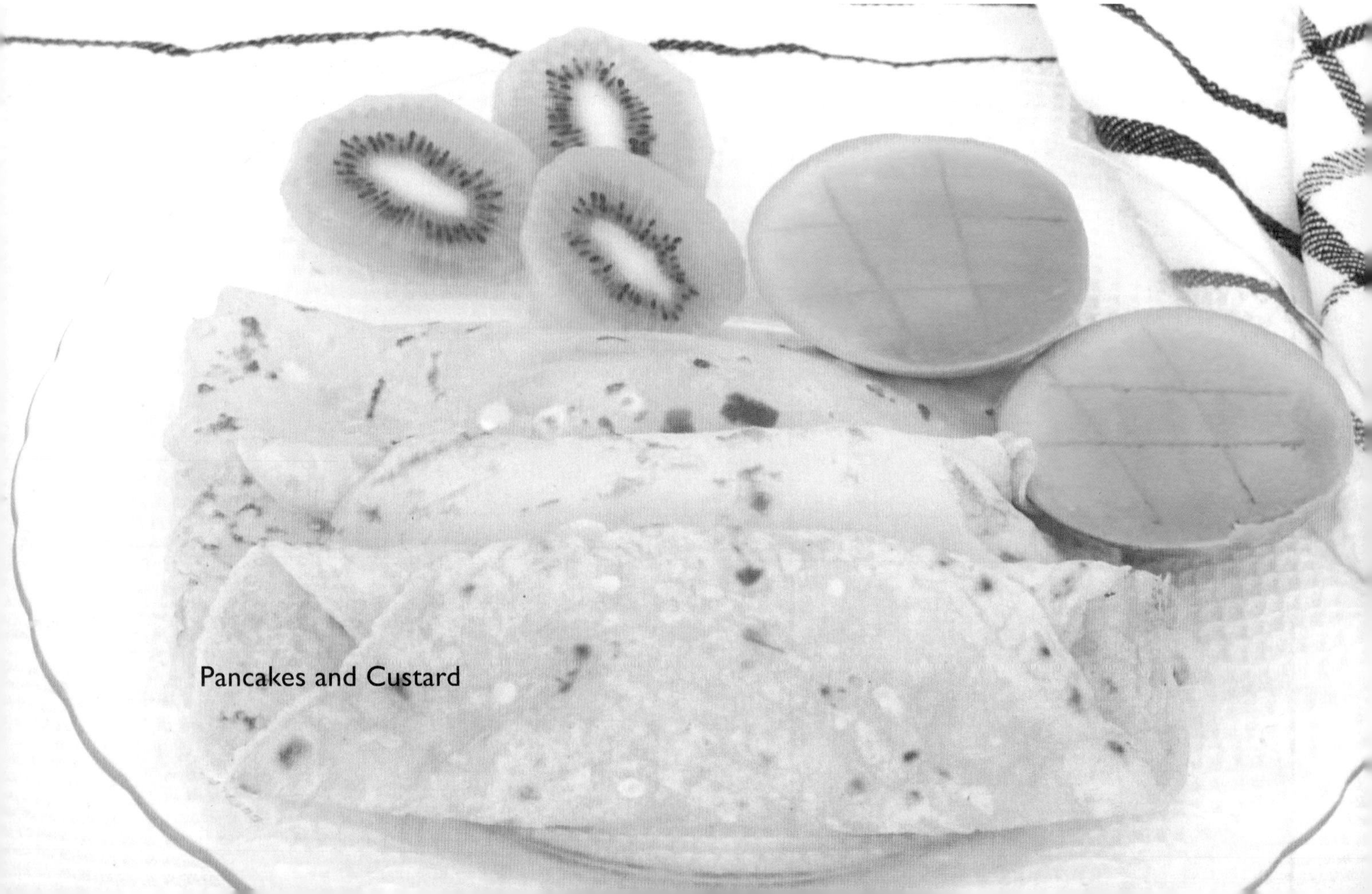

Pancakes and Custard

Banana and Raisin Fritters (Mal Poora)

A perfect treat that goes well with custard or sweetened yoghurt.

Preparation time: 20 minutes
Makes: 12 fritters

1 ½ cup (375 ml) flour
1 ½ tsp (7,5 ml) baking powder
½ tsp (2,5 ml) cinnamon powder
¼ cup (60 ml) sugar
¼ cup (60 ml) raisins
1 tsp (5 ml) vanilla essence
2 mashed bananas
Approx ¾ cup (180 ml) milk

• Sift the flour, baking powder and cinnamon
  powder together.
• Stir in the sugar, raisins and vanilla essence.

• Add the bananas and enough milk to form
  a thick batter.
• Drop tablespoons full of batter into moderate
  hot oil and deep-fry until golden brown.
• Drain well.

* *Variations: Replace the banana by ¼ cup (60 ml)*
  of mashed butternut.

Carrot Khir

Condensed milk and carrots makes a delicious dessert.

Preparation time: 45 minutes
Serves: 4 - 6 persons

8 cups (2000 ml) milk
2 cups (500 ml) grated carrots
4 opened cardamom pods
1 cinnamon stick (approx 5 cm)
¾ cup (180 ml) sugar

• Bring the milk to a gentle boil.
• Add the carrots, cardamom pods and cinnamon
  stick. Continue boiling for at least 30 minutes or
  until the mixture has reduced to half its original
  volume. Stir occasionally to prevent scorching.
• Add the sugar towards the end of the cooking.

* *Variations: Use grated calabash in place of carrots.*

Chickpea Balls (Boondia Laddoo)

Simply Wonderful

Chickpea Fudge (Besan Burfi)

Indian Doughnuts (Gulaab Jamun)

Sweets

Flaky Pastries Dipped in
Syrup (Khaja)

Milk Fudge (Burfi)

Sesame Doughnuts

Chickpea Balls (Boondia Laddoo)

In Indian homes, during Diwali, families will go to the houses of relatives and friends and exchange sweetmeats as a symbol of kindness to one another. These laddoo are traditional for such auspicious occasion.

Preparation time: 30 minutes
Makes: 12 balls

For the boondia
2 cups (500 ml) chickpea flour
Pinch of yellow food colour
¾ cup (180 ml) water
2 tbs (30 ml) raisins (optional)
½ tbs (7,5 ml) coconut for decoration

- Sift the chickpea flour and food colour together. Gradually add the water to form a thick paste.
- Press the batter into a large ladle with holes and deep-fry the pearls in very hot oil for at least 2 minutes or until slightly crisp.
- Drain and place immediately into a warm syrup for about 1 minute or until the pearls are well soaked.
- Place in a colander and allow to drain from excess syrup.
- Press the soaked pearls with your hand until the mixture holds together. Mix in the raisin.
- Roll into 12 balls and decorate with coconut.

For the syrup
1 ½ cup (375 ml) sugar
1 cup (250 ml) water

Boil the sugar and water together for 2 minutes or until the sugar dissolves.

Fresh Cheese Balls Soaked in Rose Syrup (Rasgulla)

A deliciously milk confectionery that when placed in the mouth burst with rose syrup.

Preparation time: 30 minutes
Makes: 20 balls

1 ¼ cup (310 ml) full cream milk powder
¼ cup (60 ml) flour
½ tsp (2,5 ml) bicarbonate of soda
1 tsp (5 ml) butter
Approx ¼ cup (60 ml) water

- Sift the milk powder, flour and bicarbonate together.
- Rub in the butter and gradually add enough water to form a soft dough.
- Roll into smooth, crack-free balls.
- Deep-fry over a very low heat for about 20 minutes or until the balls are a rich golden brown colour. (Gently turn the balls with a slotted spoon so that they cook evenly.)
- Drain and dip immediately into warm syrup.

For the syrup
3 cups (750 ml) water
1 ½ cups (375 ml) sugar
3 opened cardamom pods
1 tsp (5 ml) rose essence

- Boil the water, sugar and cardamom together for 1 minute.
- Stir in the rose essence.

Indian Doughnuts (Gulaab Jamun)

This is an Indian sweet that is formed into a small log, fried over a low flame, then dipped in syrup.

Preparation time: 30 minutes
Makes: 20 pieces

For the dough

1 ½ cup (375 ml) flour
½ cup (125 ml) milk powder
½ tsp (2,5 ml) bicarbonate of soda
1 tbs (15 ml) butter
¼ cup (60 ml) syrup (cooled down)
approx ⅓ cup (80 ml) water

- Sift the flour, milk powder and bicarbonate together, twice.
- Rub in the butter.
- Add the syrup and enough water to form a soft pliable dough.
- Divide the dough into 20 rounds and roll each part into about 7 cm logs.
- Deep-fry over a fairly low heat for about 10 - 12 minutes or until the gulaab jamuns are a rich dark golden brown colour.

- Drain and immediately place the hot gulaab jamuns in the warm syrup for a few moments to soak.
- Remove from the syrup and drain.

For the syrup

3 cups (750 ml) sugar
2 cups (500 ml) water

Boil the sugar and water together for 2 minutes or until the sugar dissolves and allow to cool.

Flaky Pastries Dipped in Syrup (Khaja)
An impressive sweet pastry with many layers.

Preparation time : 30 minutes
Resting time : 30 minutes
Makes : 20 pieces

1 cup (250 ml) flour
1 tbs (15 ml) butter
Approx ¼ cup (60 ml) water

Mixture to enhance layer formation
3 tbs (45 ml) oil
3 tbs (45 ml) flour

For decoration
1 tbs (15 ml) coconut

- Sift the flour, rub in the butter and add water to form a soft pliable dough.
- Cover the dough and allow to rest for 30 minutes.
- Using flour liberally, roll out into a very large paper-thin rectangle of approx 38 cm in breath and 62 cm in length.
- Spread the oil evenly on top of the pastry and sprinkle with flour.

- Roll up from the shortest side of the rectangle into a tight Swiss roll.
- Cut into 2 cm discs and roll into about 7 cm rectangles.
- Deep-fry over low heat first. Increase the heat as the pastries expand and cook until light golden brown on both sides.
- Drain well and allow to cool.
- Dip each pastry into cool syrup and place in a colander to drain excess syrup.
- Decorate with coconut.

For the syrup
1 cup (250 ml) sugar
½ cup (125 ml) water

Boil the sugar and water together for about 2 minutes or until the syrup drops from a ladle, forming a thin thread. Set aside to cool.

Milk Fudge (Burfi)

A dainty milk sweet that can be made with pretty layers of different colours.

Preparation time: 20 minutes
Setting time: 3 hours
Makes: 12 pieces

½ cup (125 ml) sugar
½ cup (125 ml) water
1 tbs (15 ml) butter
1 tsp (5 ml) vanilla essence
A drop of pink food colour
2 ½ cup (625 ml) full cream milk powder

- Bring the sugar and water to a gentle boil.
- Add the butter, vanilla essence and food colour.
- Gradually whisk in the milk powder. Turn off the heat.
- Spread the mixture onto a lightly buttered tray, into about a 1 cm thick rectangle or square.
- Make the surface of the mixture as smooth as possible with a palette knife. Add a small blob of butter while doing this as it gives a gloss touch to the burfi.
- Set for at least 3 hours before cutting into squares or diamond shapes.

Making coloured layers
Either divide the recipe into half and colour each part with a different colour. Spread the layers on top of one another.
or
Make three batches of the recipe and colour each batch separately. Pink, green and yellow are good colours to use.

For caramel burfi
- Melt the sugar until it turns light brown.
- Add the butter followed by milk instead of water.
- Whisk in the milk powder.

Coat the burfi with a layer of melted carob. For a gloss appearance add one teaspoon (5 ml) of butter to the melting carob. Sprinkle with toasted almond flakes and allow to set before cutting into desired shapes.

Caution: Carob must be melted over a double boiler, otherwise it will crumble if heated over a direct flame.

Chickpea Fudge (Besan Burfi)

A fudge-like Indian sweet made from roasted chickpea flour, nuts, coconut and raisins.

Preparation time: 20 minutes
Setting time: 3 hours
Makes: 12 pieces

¾ cup (180 ml) butter
2 cups (500 ml) chickpea flour sifted
¼ cup (60 ml) chopped unsalted nuts
¼ cup (60 ml) coconut
¼ cup (60 ml) raisins (optional)
¾ cup (180 ml) icing sugar sifted

- Melt the butter in a medium-sized heavy-based saucepan.
- Add the chickpea flour and roast until rich brown in colour. Stir often to prevent scorching.
- Add the nuts, coconut and raisins towards the end of the cooking.
- Mix in the icing sugar and turn off the heat.
- Press the mixture into a lightly greased baking tray so that it is about 1 cm thick.
- Set for at least 3 hours before cutting into squares.

* *Variations: Roll into balls instead of cutting into squares.*

SWEETS

Milk fudge samosa (Mewa Samosa)
These samosa pastries have beautiful flaky layers and a delicious burfi centre.

Preparation time: 45 minutes
Makes: 12 cakes

Step one: Preparing the filling
½ cup (125 ml) sugar
½ cup (125 ml) water
1 tbs (15 ml) butter
1 tsp (5 ml) vanilla essence
2 ¼ cup (560 ml) full cream milk powder

• Bring the sugar, water and butter to a gentle boil.
• Add the vanilla essence and whisk in the milk powder.
• Allow to cool.

Step two: Preparing the dough
2 cups (500 ml) flour
4 tbs (60 ml) sugar
2 tbs (30 ml) butter
Approx. ½ cup (125 ml) water

For the paste
¼ cup (60 ml) oil
1 tbs (15 ml) flour

• Sift the flour and stir in the sugar.
• Rub in the butter and add enough water to form a soft pliable dough.

• Roll out the dough into 2 large rounds (approx 23 cm each). (Photo 1)
• Make a paste with the oil and flour. Spread half onto one of the rounds.
• Place the other round on top of the first round and spread the remaining paste over. (Photo 2)
• Roll up tightly like a Swiss roll and allow to stand for 10 minutes. (Photo 3)

Step three: Assembling and frying
• Working from the centre to the ends, gently roll the dough so that it becomes 5 cm longer. (Photo 4&5)
• Cut into 24 discs and roll each disc into about 7 cm rounds. (Photo 6)
• Divide the filling into 12 parts and place in the centre of 12 rounds.
• Place the remaining rounds on top of the filling and seal the sides tightly by pinching them closed. Plait the edges. (Photo 7&8)
• Deep-fry in moderate hot oil until golden brown on both sides. (As the samosas cook and begin to rise to the surface, turn them over gently with a slotted ladle.)
• Drain well.

Sweet Dhal Poori (Thekwa)
Milk Fudge Samosa (Mewa Samosa)
Banana Tartlets

Sweet Dhal Poori (Thekwa)

This recipe produces a soft cake-like textured sweet poori with dhal and coconut centre.

Preparation time: 45 minutes
Makes: 10 pieces

Step one: Preparing the dough

2 cups (500 ml) flour
1 cup (250 ml) milk powder
1 tsp (5 ml) bicarbonate of soda
⅓ cup (80 ml) sugar
1 tbs (15 ml) butter
¼ tsp (1,2 ml) yellow food colour
Approx ½ cup (125 ml) water

• Sift the flour, milk powder and bicarbonate
  together.
• Stir in the sugar and rub in the butter.
• Add the food colour to the water. Then gradually
  add the water to the flour mixture to form a soft
  pliable dough.
• Knead well until smooth, cover and set aside.

Step two: Preparing the filling

½ cup (125 ml) yellow gram dhal
4 opened cardamom pods
1 tsp (5 ml) aniseed
¼ cup (60 ml) sugar
¼ cup (60 ml) coconut

• Boil the dhal until soft enough to crush between
  your fingers. Drain and grind into fine crumbs.
  (Do not add water.)
• Grind the cardamom and aniseed. Mix into
  the dhal, along with the coconut and sugar.

Step three: Assembling and frying

• Divide the dough into 10 balls.
• Pat into hat-like discs and fill each with
  a generous amount of filling. (Photo 1)
• Pinch closed.
• Gently roll out into about 10 cm rounds.
  Be careful not to make any breakages. (Photo 2)
• Deep-fry in moderate hot oil until the pooris
  balloon and are light golden brown on both
  sides. (Photo 3)
• Drain well.

Pineapple Samosa

Fruit samosas are refreshing to have with afternoon tea and can also be served as dessert.

Preparation time: 30 minutes
Makes: 6 pieces

Step one: Preparing the filling

1 small pineapple peeled and cut into small
1 cm pieces
¼ cup (60 ml) sugar
1 tbs (15 ml) butter
¼ cup (60 ml) raisins
1 small cinnamon stick (approx 3 cm)

- Simmer all ingredients together in a small heavy-based saucepan until the pineapple is soft. (Do not add water.)
- Allow the filling to cool down and remove the cinnamon stick.

Step two: Preparing the dough

1 cup (250 ml) flour
2 tbs (30 ml) sugar
1 ½ tbs (22,5 ml) butter
Approx ¼ cup (60 ml) water

- Sift the flour and stir in the sugar.
- Rub in the butter and add enough water to form a soft pliable dough.

- Divide the dough into 6 balls and roll out onto a lightly floured surface into about 6 cm rounds.

Step three: Assembling and frying

- Place about one tablespoon (15 ml) of filling in the centre of each round.
- Fold over and seal the sides either by plaiting the edges or by pressing the edges down with a fork.
- Deep-fry in moderate hot oil until golden brown.
- Drain well. Allow to cool and dust with icing sugar.

* Variations: Make custard samosas by following the custard recipe for pancakes (see page 128). Add an extra tablespoon (15 ml) of cornflour, as the custard should be thicker.
or
Using an icing nozzle, make a pattern with melted carob to decorate the samosas.

Rice Cakes (Iddly)

A special iddly mould is needed for this steamed preparation, although it can be successfully made in a small pudding bowl and turned over as a cake.

Preparation time: 10 minutes
Steaming time: 25 - 45 minutes
Makes: 6 cup cakes or 1 small 15 cm cake

1 cup (250 ml) semolina
½ cup (125 ml) full cream milk powder
2 tbs (30 ml) butter
¼ cup (60 ml) sugar
1 tsp (5 ml) baking powder
⅓ cup (80 ml) water
Coconut for decorating

- Mix all the ingredients together, except the coconut, to form a thick batter.
- Spoon into a lightly buttered iddly mould and steam for 25 minutes. If you prefer to make it in a small 15 cm wide pudding bowl, steam at least 45 minutes or until firm.
- Turn over and decorate with coconut.

Apricot Simply Wonderfuls

These delicate milk sweets require no cooking. Add dried apricots for a sweet and sour taste.

Preparation time: 15 minutes
Makes: 12 balls

1 cup (250 ml) full cream milk powder
⅓ cup (80 ml) icing sugar
1 tsp (5 ml) vanilla essence
4 tbs (60 ml) butter
2 tbs (30 ml) dried apricots cut into small pieces

• Sift the milk powder and icing sugar together.
• Add the vanilla essence and rub in enough butter so that the mixture holds together.

• Mix in the apricots.
• Roll into 12 balls.

* *Variations: Add some walnuts.*
  or
  Replace the apricots by ¼ cup (60 ml) of coconut.
  or
  1 teaspoon (5 ml) lemon zest and 1 tablespoon (15 ml) chopped nuts.
  or
  Add ¼ cup (60 ml) carob powder.

Manioc Delights

Manioc is a root vegetable that is commonly grown in tropical countries, also known as cassava. Although it can be prepared into a delicious curry, here I have used it as a sweet preparation.

Preparation time: 10 minutes
Baking time: 45 minutes
Setting time: 3 hours
Makes: 12 pieces

460 g manioc finely grated
½ cup (125 ml) sugar
¼ cup (60 ml) butter
1 tsp (5 ml) vanilla essence
½ cup (125 ml) water
Coconut for decoration

• Mix all the ingredients together except for the coconut.
• Pour into approx an 18 cm by 25 cm lightly buttered baking tray.
• Bake in a preheated moderate oven at 180° C or 350° F for about 45 minutes.
• Allow to set in the refrigerator for at least 3 hours.
• Cut into squares and roll into coconut.

Coconut Balls (Coconut Laddoo)

In the Eastern cuisine a sweet made into a ball is generally called a laddoo. This popular laddoo is made from coconut and condensed milk.

Preparation time: 15 minutes
Makes: 12 balls

2 cups (500 ml) coconut
¾ cup (180 ml) condensed milk
1 tsp (5 ml) vanilla essence
¼ cup (60 ml) raisins (optional)

• Mix all the ingredients together and roll into 12 balls.
• The balls can be refrigerated so that they firm quickly.

Malay Doughnuts

These are round spicy doughnuts which are popular amongst Cape Town's Malay population.

Preparation time: 30 minutes
Rising time: 1 ½ hours
Makes: 20 small doughnuts

2 cups (500 ml) flour
½ tsp (2,5 ml) ginger powder
½ tsp (2,5 ml) cinnamon powder
½ tsp (2,5 ml) finely grated naartjie rind
½ cup (125 ml) sugar
1 tbs (15 ml) instant yeast
2 tbs (30 ml) butter
Approx 1 cup (250 ml) warm milk
Coconut for decoration

- Sift the flour, ginger and cinnamon powder together.
- Stir in the rind, sugar and yeast.
- Rub in the butter and add enough warm milk to form a soft dough.
- Allow to rise in a warm place for about 1 hour or until double.

- Punch back the dough and form into 20 small oval shape balls.
- Place well apart on a lightly oiled tray.
- Allow to rise again for about 30 minutes.
- Deep-fry in moderate hot oil until golden brown.
- Immediately coat with syrup.
- Drain in a colander and sprinkle with coconut.

For the syrup
1 cup (250 ml) sugar
2 cups (500 ml) water

Boil the sugar and water together until a thin thread forms when poured with a ladle.

* Variations: Use ½ teaspoon (2,5 ml) crushed aniseed in place of the ginger, cinnamon and naartjie flavour.

Jam Doughnuts

Traditional American doughnuts are a great treat.

Preparation time : 20 minutes
Rising time : 1 ½ hours
Makes : 12 doughnuts

3 cups (750 ml) flour
½ cup (125 ml) sugar
1 tbs (15 ml) instant yeast
¼ cup (60 ml) butter
Approx 1 cup (250 ml) warm water
½ cup (125 ml) castor sugar
½ cup (125 ml) apricot jam

- Sift the flour and stir in the sugar and yeast.
- Rub in the butter and add enough warm water
  to form a soft pliable dough.
- Knead for 10 minutes and allow to rise in a warm
  place for about 1 hour or until double.
- Punch back the dough and form into 12 balls.
  Place well apart on a lightly oiled tray.

- Allow to rise again for about 30 minutes, then
  deep-fry in moderate hot oil until golden brown.
- Drain and roll in the castor sugar while still hot.
- Make a hole in the centre of the doughnut and
  insert jam with a nozzle or simply halve and
  sandwich with jam and freshly whipped cream.

Sesame Doughnuts

*This is the Eastern version of doughnut made into small
rounds and rolled in sesame seeds.*

Preparation time : 15 minutes
Makes : 12 balls

1 cup (250 ml) flour
1 tsp (5 ml) baking powder
¼ cup (60 ml) sugar
½ tbs (7,5 ml) butter
Approx ¼ cup (60 ml) water
2 tbs (30 ml) sesame seeds

- Sift the flour and baking powder together.
- Stir in the sugar and rub in the butter.

- Add enough water to form a soft dough.
- Divide the dough into 2 parts. Dip into the
  sesame seeds.
- Pressing firmly so that the seeds stick well onto
  the dough, roll into 12 balls.
- Deep-fry in moderate hot oil until golden brown.
- Drain well.

Dutch Koeksisters

These plaited doughnuts are a popular teatime snack in South-Africa.

Preparation time: 30 minutes
Makes: 16 pieces

2 cups (500 ml) flour
3 tsp (15 ml) baking powder
1 tbs (15 ml) sugar
1 tbs (15 ml) butter
1 tsp (5 ml) lemon juice
Approx 1 cup (250 ml) milk
Coconut for decoration

For the syrup
3 cups (750 ml) sugar
3 cups (750 ml) water
1 tsp (5 ml) ginger powder
1 cinnamon stick (approx 5 cm)
1 tbs (15 ml) golden syrup
½ tsp (2,5 ml) cream of tartar

- Sift the flour and baking powder together.
- Stir in the sugar and rub in the butter.
- Add the lemon juice and enough milk to form a soft dough.
- Roll the dough into 4 long pencil-like thick ropes. Cut into 5 cm strips. Plait 3 strips at a time and pinch the edges closed.
- Deep-fry in moderate hot oil until golden brown.
- Plunge immediately into cool syrup for about 2 minutes, then drain.
- Sprinkle with coconut.

- Boil the sugar, water, ginger powder and cinnamon stick for 5 minutes.
- Stir in the golden syrup and cream of tartar.

Biscuits, Cakes and Tarts

Basic Sponge Cakes

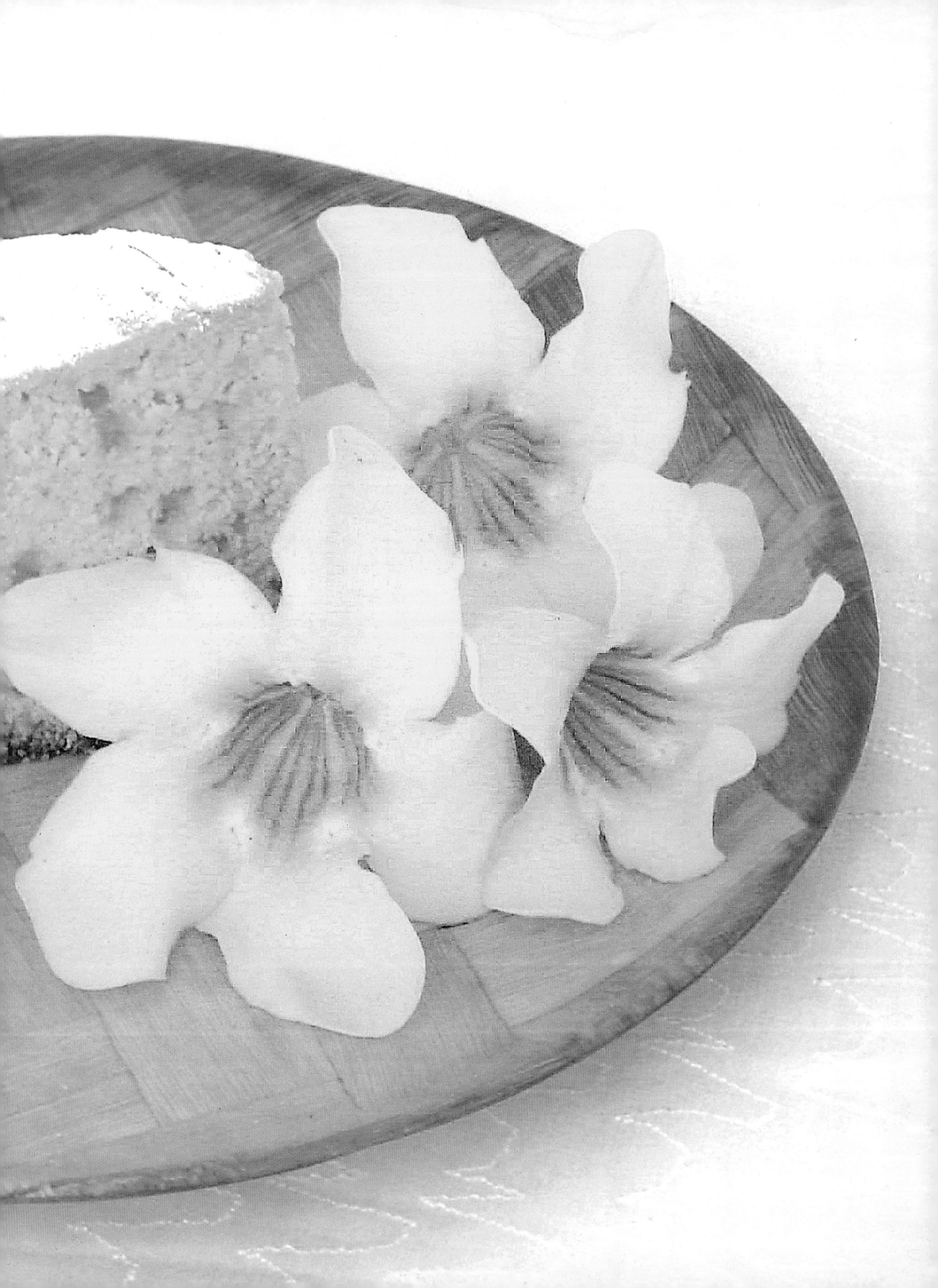

Monte Carlo's

A grand biscuit to serve at teatime.

Preparation time : 15 minutes
Baking time : 10 - 15 minutes
Makes : 12 biscuits

1 ¼ cup (310 ml) self-raising flour
¾ cup (180 ml) plain flour
½ cup (125 ml) coconut
½ cup (125 ml) brown sugar
¾ cup (180 ml) butter
1 tsp (5 ml) vanilla essence
Raspberry or strawberry jam

- Sift the flours together and stir in the coconut.
- In a separate bowl, cream the sugar, butter and vanilla essence together.
- Fold the creamed mixture into the flour to form a soft biscuit dough.
- Roll into 24 balls. Place well apart on a lightly greased baking tray and flatten with a fork.
- Bake in a preheated moderate oven at 180° C or 350° F for about 10 - 15 minutes or until the biscuit is light golden brown underneath.

- Allow to cool and sandwich together with jam and creamy icing.

For the creamy icing
¾ cup (180 ml) icing sugar
¼ cup (60 ml) butter
½ tsp (2,5 ml) vanilla essence
2 tsp (10 ml) milk

Sift the icing sugar and add the rest of the ingredients to form a creamy mixture.

Hint: Self raising flour can be made by adding 1 ¼ cup flour (310 ml) with 1 ¼ tsp (6,2 ml) baking powder.

Romany Creams

A delicious biscuit made with carob instead of chocolate. Carob is a healthy substitute of chocolate because it is caffeine-free.

Preparation time : 15 minutes
Baking time : 10 -15 minutes
Makes : 12 biscuits

2 cups (500 ml) flour
2 tsp (10 ml) baking powder
1 tbs (15 ml) carob powder
1 ½ cup (375 ml) coconut
1 cup (125 ml) butter
½ cup (125 ml) castor sugar
1 tsp (5 ml) vanilla essence
¼ cup (60 ml) milk if necessary

- Sift the flour, baking powder and carob powder together.
- Stir in the coconut.
- Cream the butter, sugar and vanilla essence together.

- Fold the creamed mixture into the flour to form a soft biscuit dough. Add milk if necessary.
- Roll into 24 balls and place well apart onto a lightly greased baking tray.
- Press with a fork and bake in a preheated moderate oven at 180° C or 350° F for about 10 - 15 minutes or until light golden brown underneath.
- Allow to cool and sandwich together with creamy icing as above (see Monte Carlo's), but add 1 teaspoon (5 ml) carob powder.

Napolitaine

A popular French biscuit, when shaped in hearts will make a perfect gift.

Preparation time: 15 minutes
Baking time: 10 -15 minutes
Makes: 12 heart shaped biscuits

Basic biscuit recipe

1 ½ cup (375 ml) flour
½ cup (125 ml) cornflour
½ cup (125 ml) icing sugar
1 tsp (5 ml) vanilla essence
¾ cup (180 ml) butter
Approx 2 tbs (30 ml) strawberry jams
for the centres

- Sift the flour, cornflour and icing sugar together.
- Add the vanilla essence and rub in the butter to form a soft biscuit dough.
- Roll out on a lightly floured surface into 1 cm thick rectangle.
- Cut out heart shapes with a biscuit cutter or any other shape as desired and place on a lightly greased baking tray.
- Bake in a preheated moderate oven at 180° C or 350° F for about 10 -15 minutes or until the biscuits are light golden brown underneath.

- Allow to cool and sandwich together with strawberry jam.
- Spread the tops with glaze icing, which will harden as the icing sets.

For the glaze icing

½ cup (125 ml) sifted icing sugar
A drop of pink colour
2 tsp (10 ml) water

Mix all the ingredients together to form a smooth paste.

Easy Melts

A simple biscuit to prepare for afternoon tea.

Preparation time: 15 minutes
Baking time: 15 - 20 minutes
Refrigeration time: 20 minutes
Makes: 12 biscuits

1 cup (250 ml) flour
⅓ cup (80 ml) cornflour
¼ cup (60 ml) castor sugar
½ cup (125 ml) butter

- Sift the flour and cornflour together.
- Add the sugar and rub in the butter to form a soft biscuit dough.

- Roll the dough into an approx 18 cm sausage.
- Place in the fridge for 20 minutes.
- Cut into 1 cm discs and place well apart on a lightly greased tray.
- Bake in a preheated moderate oven at 180° C or 350° F for about 15 - 20 minutes or until light golden brown underneath.

Date Crescents, Carob Chip Cookies, Éclair Biscuits and Sesame Biscuits

The basic biscuit recipe from Napolitaine forms the basis of these four biscuits.

Preparation time: 15 minutes
Baking time: 10 - 15 minutes
Makes: approx 12 biscuits

Date crescents

- Follow the basic biscuit recipe from Napolitaine biscuits.(see page 147)
- Make a filling by heating and mashing ½ cup (125 ml) dates (without seeds) with 1 teaspoon (5 ml) of lemon juice.
- Roll into 12 small balls.
- Divide the biscuit dough into 12 parts and mould around the date balls.
- Form into moon crescent shapes.
- Bake in a preheated moderate oven at 180° C or 350° F for about 10 - 15 minutes or until light golden brown underneath.
- Dust liberally with icing sugar while warm.

Carob chip cookies

- Follow the basic dough recipe from the Napolitaine biscuits. (see page 147)
- Add ½ cup (125 ml) carob chunks to the dough.
- Form into 12 rounds and bake in a preheated moderate oven at 180° C or 350° F for about 10 - 15 minutes or until light brown underneath.
- Allow to cool.
- Melt a small block of carob in a double boiler and stir in 1 teaspoon (5 ml) butter.
- Dip each biscuit in the carob so that one third of the shape is coated.
- Place on a rack until the carob hardens.

Éclair biscuits

- Follow the basic biscuit recipe from the Napolitaine biscuits. (see page 147)
- Using a 1 ½ cm icing nozzle make about 24 logs (approx 7 cm each).
- Bake in a preheated moderate oven at 180° C or 350° F for about 10 - 15 minutes or until light golden brown underneath. Allow to cool.
- Sandwich together with basic butter icing as in creamy icing for Monte Carlo's. (see page 146)
- Dip the sides in melted carob and place on a rack to harden.

Sesame biscuits

- Add ¼ cup (60 ml) toasted sesame seeds to the basic Napolitaine biscuit dough. (see page 147)
- Divide the dough into about 18 parts and roll into balls.
- Place each ball into a petite cup cake case and bake in a preheated moderate oven at 180° C or 350° F for about 10 - 15 minutes or until light golden brown underneath. Allow to cool.
- Coat the tops with melted carob and place a silver ball in the centre of each biscuit.

Cardamom Biscuits (Naankatia)

A popular biscuit served traditionally in Eastern homes.

Preparation time: 15 minutes
Baking time: 15 - 20 minutes
Makes: 12 biscuits

1 cup (250 ml) flour
½ tsp (2,5 ml) bicarbonate of soda
½ tsp (2,5 ml) cardamom powder
½ tsp (2,5 ml) ground nutmeg
½ cup (125 ml) castor sugar
½ cup (125 ml) ghee

- Sift flour and bicarbonate together.
- Add cardamom powder, nutmeg and sugar.
- Rub in ghee to form a soft biscuit dough.
- Form into 12 large biscuits and place well apart on a lightly greased baking tray.
- Bake in a preheated moderate oven at 180° C or 350° F for about 15 - 20 minutes or until light golden brown underneath.

Crunchies (Oat Biscuit)

A healthy oats and coconut biscuit that can be served anytime of the day.

Preparation time: 15 minutes
Baking time: 20 - 25 minutes
Makes: approx 12 biscuits

1 cup (250 ml) flour
2 cups (500 ml) oats
1 cup (250 ml) coconut
1 cup (250 ml) sugar
1 cup (250 ml) butter
1 tbs (15 ml) golden syrup
1 tsp (5 ml) bicarbonate of soda

- Sift flour into a bowl. Gently mix in the oats, coconut and sugar.
- Melt the butter in a heavy-based saucepan and keep over low heat.
- Stir in the bicarbonate. When the mixture begins to froth turn off the heat.
- Add the golden syrup and fold the mixture into the dry ingredients.
- Place in approx a 20 cm by 25 cm lightly greased baking try and bake in a preheated moderate oven at 180° C or 350° F for about 20 - 25 minutes or until light golden brown.
- Cut into squares while still hot.
- Allow to cool before removing the biscuit from the tray.

Crunchies (Oat Biscuit)

Basic Sponge Cake

This recipe is very versatile as a variety of flavours and fruit can be added. Try adding bananas, mixed spices, passion fruit, orange zest or a handful of dates.

Preparation time : 15 minutes
Baking time : 30 minutes
Makes : one 20 cm cake

3 cups (750 ml) flour
4 tsp (20 ml) baking powder
2 tbs (30 ml) cornflour
½ cup (125 ml) butter
1 cup (250 ml) sugar
1 tbs (15 ml) lemon juice
Pinch of yellow food colour [optional]
1 tsp (5 ml) vanilla essence
Approx 2 cups (500 ml) milk

- Sift the flour, baking powder and cornflour together.
- In a separate bowl, cream the butter and sugar together.
- Add the lemon juice, food colour and vanilla essence.
- Fold into the dry ingredients along with the milk to form a thick batter.
- Divide the mixture into 2 lightly greased 20 cm cake tins and bake in a preheated moderate oven at 180° C or 350° F for about 30 minutes or until firm.
- Allow the cake to cool before removing from the tins.
- Sandwich together and decorate with butter icing.

Butter icing
1 ½ cups (375 ml) icing sugar
4 tbs (60 ml) butter
1 tsp (5 ml) vanilla essence
2 tsp (10 ml) milk

- Sift the icing sugar.
- Add the remaining ingredients and cream together until light and fluffy.

* Variations: Decrease the milk of the cake batter by ½ cup (125 ml) and add 1 cup (250 ml) of roughly chopped dried fruit to the mixture.
or
Sandwich with custard or caramel and decorate with butter icing. Sprinkle with finely chopped nuts.

Black Forest Cake

A wonderful rich cake that is decorated with slightly sweetened fresh cream and red cherries or strawberries.

Preparation time: 15 minutes
Baking time: 30 minutes
Makes: one 20 cm cake

2 ½ cups (625 ml) flour
3 tsp (15 ml) baking powder
½ cup (125 ml) butter
1 ¼ cups (310 ml) sugar
1 tbs (15 ml) lemon juice
1 tsp (5 ml) vanilla essence
1 cup (250 ml) carob powder
¼ cup (60 ml) hot water
Approx 1 ¼ cup (310 ml) milk

- Sift the flour and baking powder together.
- In a separate bowl, cream the butter, sugar, lemon juice and vanilla essence together.
- Make a paste with the carob powder and hot water. Add to the creamed mixture along with the milk.
- Fold all the ingredients together to form a thick batter.

- Divide the batter into 2 lightly greased 20 cm cake tins and bake in a preheated moderate oven at 180° C or 350° F for about 30 minutes or until firm.
- Allow the cakes to cool before removing them from the tins.

For decoration
2 tbs (30 ml) strawberry jam
1 cup (250 ml) fresh cream
1 tbs (30 ml) sugar
1 tsp (5 ml) vanilla essence
Red cherries or strawberries
Grated carob

- Sandwich the cake with strawberry jam.
- Whip the cream, sugar and vanilla essence together to a soft peak stage.
- Ice the cake with the cream and decorate with red cherries or strawberries and carob as desired.

Black Forest Cake

Carrot Cake with Cream Cheese Topping
A moist carrot cake with nuts and fruit.

Preparation time: 15 minutes
Baking time: 45 minutes
Makes: one 20 cm cake

2 ½ cups (625 ml) flour
½ tsp (2,5 ml) bicarbonate of soda
2 tsp (10 ml) baking powder
1 tsp (5 ml) cinnamon powder
½ tsp (2,5 ml) nutmeg
1 tsp (5 ml) ground cloves
1 ½ cup (375 ml) oil
1 ¾ cup (430 ml) sugar
2 cups (500 ml) grated carrots
1 cup (250 ml) yoghurt
¼ cup (60 ml) raisins (optional)
¼ cup (60 ml) nuts (optional)

- Sift the first six ingredients together.
- In a separate bowl, mix the oil, sugar, carrots, yoghurt, raisins and nuts together.
- Fold into the dry ingredients to form a thick batter.
- Line a 20 cm cake tin with greaseproof paper and lightly grease.

- Pour the cake batter into the cake tin and bake in a preheated moderate oven at 180° C or 350° F for about 45 minutes or until firm.
- Allow the cakes to cool before removing them from the tins.

Cream cheese icing
1 cup (250 ml) cream cheese
¼ cup (60 ml) icing sugar
1 tsp (5 ml) vanilla essence
1 tsp (5 ml) finely grated orange rind
Walnuts
Cherries

- Mix the cream cheese, icing sugar, vanilla essence and orange rind together.
- Spread on top of the cake and decorate with walnuts and cherries.

Banana and Nut Loaf
A wonderful banana and nut loaf to bake for tea time.

Preparation time: 15 minutes
Baking time: 45 minutes
Makes: one loaf

2 cups (500 ml) flour
3 tsp (15 ml) baking powder
½ tsp (2,5 ml) cinnamon powder
½ cup (125 ml) butter
¾ cup (180 ml) brown sugar
1 tsp (5 ml) vanilla essence
4 tbs (60 ml) yoghurt
3 mashed bananas
½ cup (125 ml) chopped nut

- Sift the flour, baking powder and cinnamon powder together.

- In a separate bowl, cream the butter, sugar, vanilla essence, yoghurt and bananas together. Add the chopped nuts.
- Fold all the ingredients together to form a thick batter.
- Place in a lightly greased loaf tin and bake in a preheated moderate oven at 180° C or 350° F for about 45 minutes or until firm.
- Allow to cool before removing from the tin.

Fruit Cake with Apricot Glaze

Not all cakes need elaborate decorations. A simple glaze finish is enough
to enhance this delicious fruit cake.

Preparation time: 15 minutes
Baking time: 1 hour
Makes: one 20 cm cake

2 ½ (625 ml) cups flour
3 tsp (15 ml) baking powder
½ tsp (2,5 ml) mixed spice
½ tsp (2,5 ml) ground nutmeg
½ tsp (2,5 ml) cinnamon powder
¼ cup (60 ml) carob powder (optional)
1 ½ (350 ml) cups sugar
½ cup (125 ml) butter
1 tsp (5 ml) vanilla essence
1 tbs (15 ml) lemon juice
1 cup (250 ml) fruit mix
¼ cup (60 ml) red cherries
1 - 1 ¼ cups (250 ml - 310 ml) milk

- Sift the first six ingredients together.
- In a separate bowl, cream the sugar, butter, vanilla essence and lemon juice together. Add the fruit mix and red cherries.
- Fold into the dry ingredients along with the milk to form a thick batter.

- Line a 20 cm cake tin that is about 7 cm deep with greaseproof paper and lightly grease.
- Pour the cake batter into the tin, flatten with a palette knife and bake in a preheated moderate oven at 180° C or 350° F for about 45 minutes or until firm.
- Remove the cake from the tin and allow to cool before applying the glaze.

For the apricot glace

1 tsp (5 ml) cornflour
3 tbl (45 ml) water
3 tbs (45 ml) apricot jam
1 tsp (5 ml) lemon juice

- Make a paste with the cornflour and water. Add to the jam.
- Heat in a small saucepan, stirring continuously until the mixture thickens.
- Mix in the lemon juice.
- Allow to cool slightly, then brush over the fruit cake.

Aunty Felia's Date Loaf

Here is a delicious recipe that has been handed down to me by my aunty Rita.
This was her late sister's famous recipe.

Preparation time: 15 minutes
Baking time: 1 hour
Makes: one loaf

½ cup (125 ml) or 125 g butter
1 cup (250 ml) sugar
1 tsp (5 ml) bicarbonate of soda
Approx 450 g dates without seeds
1 ½ cups (375 ml) boiling water
3 cups (750 ml) self raising flour
1 tsp (5 ml) cinnamon powder
½ tsp (2,5 ml) ginger powder
½ tsp (2,5 ml) mixed spice
Pinch of salt

- Cream the butter, sugar and bicarbonate together.
- Soak the dates in the water and add to the creamy mixture.
- Sift the rest of the dry ingredients together.
- Fold in the creamy mixture.
- Place into a greased loaf tin.
- Bake in a preheated moderate oven at 190° C or 375° F for about 1 hour or until firm.
- Allow to cool before removing from the tin.

Fairy Cup Cakes

Fairy cup cakes are very popular for children's birthday parties. Here is an eggless recipe for these well liked cakes.

Preparation time: 15 minutes
Baking time: 15 minutes
Makes: 12 cupcakes

1 ¾ cups (430 ml) flour
1 ½ tsp (7,5 ml) baking powder
½ cup (125 ml) butter
½ cup (125 ml) sugar
1 tbs (15 ml) yoghurt
1 tsp (5 ml) vanilla essence
Approx ¾ (180 ml) cup milk

• Sift the flour and baking powder together.
• In a separate bowl, cream the butter, sugar, yoghurt and vanilla essence together.
• Fold into the dry ingredients along with the milk to form a thick batter.

• Divide the mixture into 12 cupcake cases and bake in a preheated moderate oven at 190° C or 375° F for about 15 minutes or until light golden brown.
• Allow to cool before removing from the tray.
• Decorate with butter icing, hundreds and thousands and glazed cherries or as desired. (See page 150 for butter icing.)

Baked Cheese Cake

Here is a gelatine-free cheesecake recipe that can be made with curd or tofu.

Preparation time: 30 minutes
Baking time: 45 minutes
Refrigeration time: 3 hours
Makes: one 23 cm cake

Step one: Preparing the dough
2 cups (500 ml) flour
½ cup (125 ml) sugar
¼ cup (60 ml) butter
Approx ½ cup (125 ml) water

- Sift the flour, stir in the sugar and rub in the butter.
- Add enough water to form a soft pliable dough.
- Press into a lightly greased 23 cm cheesecake mould.

Step two: Preparing the filling, assembling and baking
3 cups (750 ml) curd or tofu
¼ cup (60 ml) butter
¼ cup (60 ml) oil

1 cup (250 ml) sugar
2 tsp (10 ml) vanilla essences
¼ cup (60 ml) lemon juice

- Blend the curd or tofu, butter, oil, sugar and vanilla essence together.
- Gradually add the lemon juice until the mixture thickens.
- Pour into the pastry case.
- Bake in a preheated moderate oven at 180° C or 350° F for about 45 minutes or until golden brown on top.
- Refrigerate for at least 3 hours before serving.

Serving suggestion: Decorate with slightly sweetened freshly whipped cream and strawberries.

Banana Tartlets

Individual tarts with banana filling that can also be made into one large tart.

Preparation time: 30 minutes
Baking time: 30 minutes
Makes: 6 tartlets

Step one: Preparing the dough
1 cup (250 ml) flour
2 tbs (30 ml) sugar
1 tbs (15 ml) butter
Approx ¼ cup (60 ml) water

- Sift the flour and stir in the sugar.
- Rub in the butter and add enough water to from a soft pliable dough.

Step two: Preparing the filling
1 tbs (15 ml) butter
4 large bananas peeled and mashed
2 tbs (30 ml) sugar

- Melt the butter in a small saucepan.

- Add the bananas and sugar. Cook for about 5 minutes.
- Allow to cool.

Step three: Assembling and baking
- Divide the dough into half.
- Using half the dough, divide into 6 balls and roll out into approx 10 cm rounds.
- Grease a cup cake tray and line with the rounds.
- Fill each with a generous amount of banana filling.
- Roll out the remaining dough into a rectangle and cut approx 1 cm by 3 cm strips.
- Cover each tart with 4 strips crossing over one another.
- Glaze with milk and bake in a preheated moderate oven at 180° C or 350° F for about 30 minutes or until rich golden brown in colour.
- Allow the tarts cool slightly before removing from the tray.

Sweet Potato Cake

A wheat-free cake that uses sweet potato as its main ingredient.

Preparation time: 20 minutes
Baking time: 30 minutes
Makes: one 20 cm cake

2 cups (500 ml) full cream milk powder
1 tsp (5 ml) baking powder
1 tsp (5 ml) cardamom powder
1 cup (250 ml) coconut
¼ cup (60 ml) toasted almonds cut into halves
2 medium sweet potatoes (approx 300 g) boiled,
peeled and mashed

• Sift the milk powder, baking powder and cardamom
  powder together.

• Stir in the coconut and almonds.
• Add the mash potato to form a thick batter.
• Spoon into a greased 20 cm cake tin and bake
  in a preheated moderate oven at 180° C or 350° F
  for about 30 minutes or until firm.

Serving suggestion: This cake does not require icing
as it is wonderful on its own.

Apple Tart

Grandma's favourite apple tart recipe.

Preparation time: 20 minutes
Baking time: 20 - 30 minutes
Makes: one 20 cm tart

Step one: Preparing the filling
4 large sour green apples
1 cup (250 ml) water
2 tbs (30 ml) butter
½ cup (125 ml) sugar
1 small cinnamon stick (approx 5 cm)
2 tbs (30 ml) cornflour

• Peel the apple and cut into thin slices.
• Stew in a small heavy-based saucepan with
  ½ cup (125 ml) of the water, butter, sugar
  and cinnamon stick.
• Make a paste with the remaining water
  and cornflour. Add to the apples
  to thicken.
• Set aside to cool.

Step two: Preparing the dough
1 cup (250 ml) flour
½ cup (125 ml) coconut
4 tbs (60 ml) sugar
¼ cup (60 ml) butter
Milk for glazing

• Sift flour and stir in coconut and sugar.
• Rub in butter to form a soft dough.
• Roll three quarter of the dough into a large round
  and press into a lightly greased 20 cm tart dish.
• Fill with the stewed apples.
• Coarsely grate the remaining dough and cover
  the top of the tart. Glaze with milk.
• Bake in a preheated moderate oven at 190° C
  or 375° F for about 20 - 30 minutes or until golden
  brown on top.

Serving suggestion: Serve with custard or slightly
sweetened fresh cream.

Milk Tart

This dish is very popular amongst South Africans where it is known in Afrikaans as 'melktert'.

Preparation time : 20 minutes
Baking time : 30 minutes
Setting time : 1 hour
Makes : one 20 cm tart

Step one : Preparing the base

1 cup (250 ml) flour
1 tsp (5 ml) baking powder
¼ cup (60 ml) sugar
¼ cup (60 ml) butter
Approx ¼ cup (60 ml) water

- Sift the flour and baking powder together.
- Stir in the sugar and rub in the butter.
- Add enough water to form a soft pliable dough.
- Roll out into a large round and press into a lightly greased 20 cm tart dish.
- Blind bake for 10 minutes.

Step two : Preparing the filling, assembling and baking

2 cups (500 ml) milk
1 small cinnamon stick (approx 5 cm)
2 tbs (30 ml) butter

¼ cup (60 ml) sugar
4 tbs (60 ml) cornflour
2 tbs (30 ml) cake flour
1 tsp (5 ml) cinnamon powder for sprinkling

- Bring 1 ½ cups (375 ml) of the milk to boil and allow to simmer along with the cinnamon stick, butter and sugar.
- Make a paste with the remaining milk, cornflour and cake flour. Add to the simmering milk. Stir continuously until the mixture thickens.
- Remove the cinnamon stick and pour into the pastry mould.
- Sprinkle with cinnamon powder.
- Bake in a preheated moderate oven at 190° C or 375° for about 30 minutes or until the sides of the pastry is golden brown.
- Place in the refrigerator to set for at least 1 hour before serving.

Beverages

Fresh Lemon Juice
Mango Yoghurt Shake
Rose Flavoured Milkshake (Falooda)
Tamarind Juice

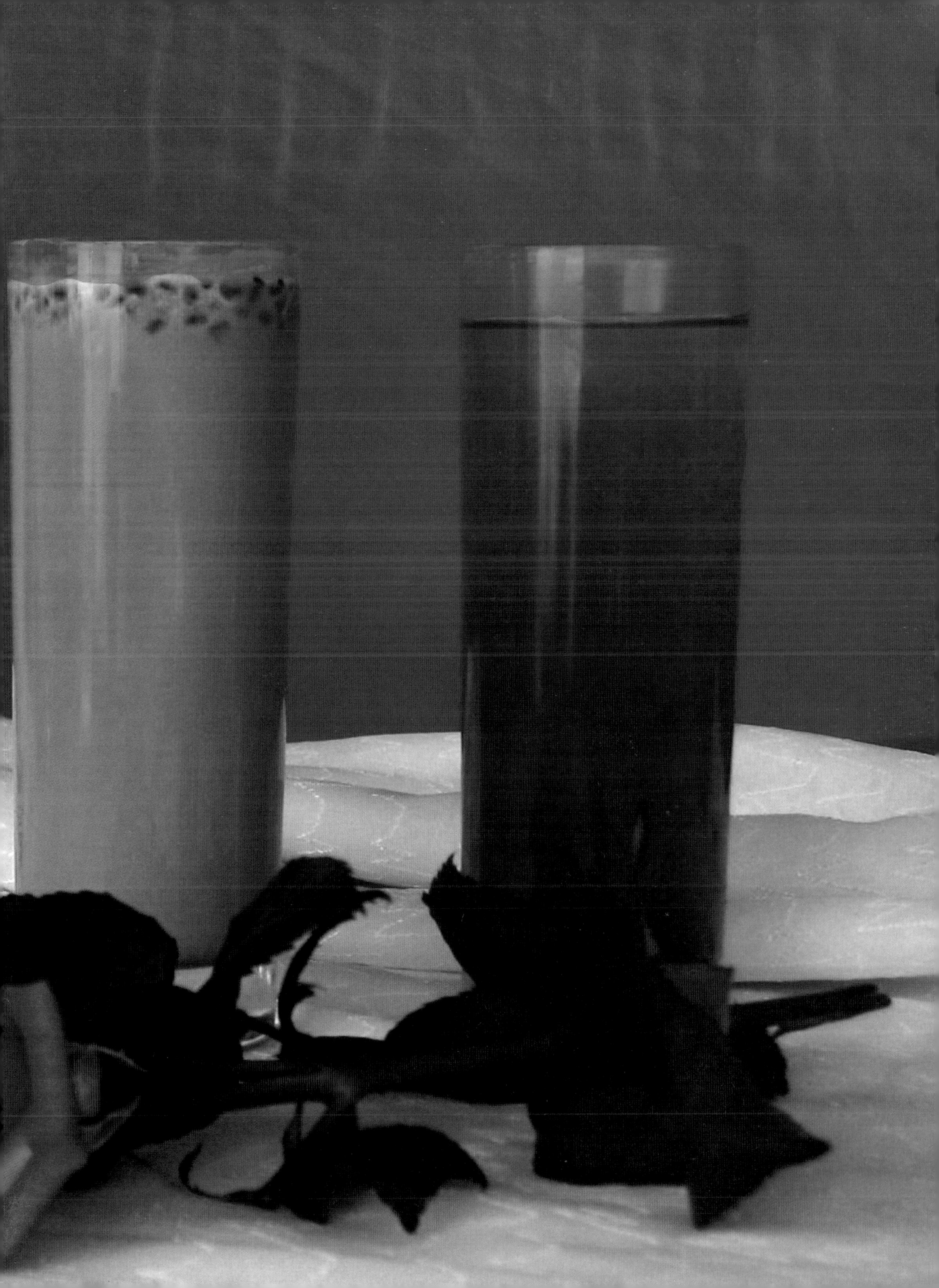

BEVERAGES

Fresh Fruit Juice

Fresh fruit juice makes an ideal breakfast appetizer. For a light refreshing drink, serve in tall glasses with ice cubes and orange wedges.

Preparation time: 10 minutes
Makes: 1 litre

1 pear
Juice of 2 oranges freshly squeezed
2 bananas
1 apple
¾ cup (180 ml) sugar
4 cup (1000 ml) water

- Blend all the ingredients together.
- Chill before serving.

* Variations: Replace any of the fruit with a small mango, papaya, kiwi fruit or some strawberries.

Tropical Fruit Punch

A non-alcoholic cocktail drink with a delightful fruit combination.

Preparation time: 10 minutes
Makes: 1 ½ litres

2 cups (500 ml) naturally sweetened pineapple juice
(available in commercial stores)
2 cups (500 ml) naturally sweetened passion fruit juice
(available in commercial stores)
2 cups (500 ml) fizzy cold drink (white colour)

- Mix the juices together.
- Allow to chill.
- Add the fizzy cold drink just before serving.

Watermelon and Strawberry Punch

While your guests are relaxing before the meal, impress them with this exotic fruit punch.

Preparation time: 10 minutes
Makes: approx 1 litre

1 watermelon
1 cup (250 ml) naturally sweetened fruit juice
(available in commercial stores)
1 ripe yellow melon
2 cups (500 ml) fizzy cold drink
(red or white colour)
Strawberries
A few fresh mint leaves

- Halve a large watermelon, scoop out the centre and fill with the following tropical fruit punch.
- Mix together naturally sweetened commercial fruit juice, some pulp from the watermelon and yellow melon.
- Add the fizzy cold drink, some sliced strawberries and garnish with mint leaves.

Fresh Lemon Juice

This lemon water makes a perfect afternoon thirst quencher.

Preparation time: 10 minutes
Makes: 1 litre

4 cups (1000 ml) water
2 tbs (30 ml) of freshly squeezed lemon juice
¼ cup (60 ml) sugar
Pinch of black pepper (optional)
1 tsp (5 ml) rose essence (optional)
4 rose petals (optional)

- Blend all the ingredients together except for the rose petals.
- Allow to chill.
- Garnish with rose petals before serving.

Tamarind Juice

Serve this sweet and sour tropical drink with crushed ice on a hot summer day.

Preparation time: 10 minutes
Makes: 1 litre

2 tbs (30 ml) tamarind pulp
4 cups (1000 ml) water
4 tbs (60 ml) sugar or honey

- Soak the tamarind in one cup (250 ml) of the water. Strain from pips.
- Mix the tamarind water with the remaining liquid and sweetener.
- Serve chilled.

Orange and Whey Refresher

While making homemade cheese, save the whey for making this beverage, as it is very nutritious.

Preparation time: 10 minutes
Makes: 1 litre

4 cups (1000 ml) whey
Juice from 4 oranges
4 tbs (60 ml) sugar or honey

Whisk all the ingredients together and place in the fridge until cold.

BEVERAGES

Rose Flavoured Milkshake (Falooda)

This gentle drink is infused with rose essence and is prefect for celebrations.

Preparation time: 10 minutes
Makes: 1 litre

4 cups (1000 ml) milk
¼ cup (60 ml) sugar
Few drops of pink food colour
1 tsp (5 ml) rose essence
1 tsp (5 ml) tookmaria seeds (also known as falooda seeds)
¼ cup (60 ml) vegetarian jelly finely grated

• Blend the milk and sugar together.
• Add enough food colour to make a deep pink milk.
• Stir in the rose essence and tookmaria seeds.
• Chill and pour into individual glasses.
• Add about a tablespoon (15 ml) of jelly to each glass.

For the vegetarian jelly
½ cup (125 ml) water
1 tsp (5 ml) agar-agar (china grass)
1 tbs (15 ml) sugar
1 drop of green food colour

• Mix all the ingredients together and bring to boil in a small saucepan.
• Place in the fridge to set. Finely grate.

Serving suggestion: Decorate with toasted slivers of blanched almonds.

* Variations: Add ice cream and raspberry fizzy cold drink before serving.
or
Rose essence can be replaced by 1 teaspoon (5 ml) of vanilla essence.

Banana Smoothie

An energizing milkshake that is easy to prepare.

Preparation time: 10 minutes
Makes: 1 litre

4 cups (1000 ml) milk
4 tbs (60 ml) sugar or honey
2 tsp (10 ml) vanilla essence
4 mashed bananas

• Blend all the ingredients together until smooth.
• Chill before serving.

* Variations: Use mango, apple, pear or ¼ cup (60 ml) carob powder instead of banana.

Avocado and Coconut Milkshake

This is a popular Indian milk shake.

Preparation time: 10 minutes
Makes: 1 litre

1 ripe avocado
4 cups (1000 ml) milk
4 tbs (60 ml) sugar or honey
2 tsp (10 ml) vanilla essence
1 tbs (15 ml) coconut

• Blend all the ingredients together.
• Chill and pour into glasses.

Papaya or Mango Yoghurt Shake

A yoghurt drink that is also known as lassi.

Preparation time: 10 minutes
Makes: 1 ½ litres

2 cups (500 ml) yoghurt
2 cups (500 ml) water
The pulp from one large mango or one small papaya
½ cup (125 ml) sugar
2 tsp (10 ml) vanilla essence

- Blend all the ingredients together until smooth.
- Chill before serving.

* Variations: Instead of using fruit and vanilla, add 1 teaspoon (5 ml) rose essence and garnish with rose petals.

Yogi Tea

Serve this tea for a festive occasion during cold weather.

Preparation time: 10 minutes
Makes: 4 cups

2 cups (500 ml) milk
2 cups (500 ml) water
2 rooibos tea bags
1 cinnamon stick (approx 5 cm)
1 tbs (15 ml) finely grated ginger
4 tbs (60 ml) honey or sugar

- Boil the milk, water and tea bags together.
- Add the cinnamon stick and ginger. Allow to simmer over a low heat for about 2 minutes so that the flavours can be absorbed.
- Add the sweetener to taste.
- Strain before serving.

* Variations: Replace the ginger by three opened cardamom pods

Ayurvedic Tea

A natural tea that contains no tannin or caffeine.

Preparation time: 15 minutes
Makes: 4 cups

1 cinnamon stick (approx 5 cm)
¼ tsp (1,2 ml) freshly ground nutmeg
¼ tsp (1,2 ml) aniseed
¼ tsp (1,2 ml) saffron threads
4 opened cardamom pods
4 cloves
½ tsp (2,5 ml) freshly grated ginger
4 cups (1000 ml) milk
4 tbs (60 ml) sugar or honey

- Grind all the spices together into a fine powder.
- Boil the milk and add the spices.
- Allow to simmer for two minutes so that the flavours can be absorbed.
- Add the sweetener to taste.
- Strain before serving.

BEVERAGES

Iced Lemon Tea

Featuring rooibos tea that is low in tannin and is caffeine-free.

Preparation time: 10 minutes
Makes: 1 ½ litres

4 cups (1000 ml) water
2 rooibos tea bags
4 tbs (60 ml) sugar or honey
1 small bottle ginger ale
Ice cubes
1 small lemon thinly sliced

- Boil the water and add the tea bags.
- Stir in the sweetener and place in the refrigerator until cold.
- Just before serving add the ginger ale, ice cubes and garnish with lemon slices.

Toasted Almond and Nutmeg Milk

This warm drink is most comforting at the end of a tiring day.

Preparation time: 10 minutes
Makes: 4 mugs

4 cups (1000 ml) milk
½ tsp (2,5 ml) freshly ground nutmeg
½ tsp (2,5 ml) cinnamon powder
4 tbs (60 ml) sugar or honey
¼ cup (60 ml) slivered almonds lightly toasted

- Bring the milk to a gentle boil.
- Add the nutmeg, cinnamon powder and allow to simmer for two minutes.
- Add the sweetener to taste.
- Garnish with almonds.

Banana and Cinnamon Milk

A nourishing drink that is ideal for the morning.

Preparation time: 10 minutes
Makes: 4 mugs

4 cups (1000 ml) milk
1 cinnamon stick (approx 5 cm)
½ tsp (2,5 ml) ground nutmeg
1 tbs (15 ml) butter
4 mashed bananas
4 tbs (60 ml) sugar or honey

- Bring the milk, cinnamon stick and nutmeg to a gentle boil and allow to simmer for two minutes.
- Add the butter, bananas and sweetener to taste.
- Remove the cinnamon stick before serving.
- Best served hot.

Ginger and Turmeric Milk

A healthy milk drink that detoxifies the body and is also good for colds.

Preparation time: 10 minutes
Makes: 4 mugs

4 cups (1000 ml) milk
1 tbs (15 ml) finely grated ginger
1 tsp (5 ml) turmeric powder
4 tbs (60 ml) sugar or honey

• Bring the milk to a gentle boil.
• Add the ginger and turmeric powder. Allow to simmer for two minutes so that the flavours can be absorbed.
• Add the sweetener to taste.
• Strain before serving.

Sago Milk

A non-grain milk beverage; with the addition of raisins this preparation can also be served as a pudding.

Preparation time: 10 - 15 minutes
Soaking time: 30 minutes
Makes: 4 mugs

¼ cup (60 ml) unsoaked sago
4 cups (1000 ml) milk
4 opened cardamom pods
1 cinnamon stick (approx 5 cm)
4 tbs (60 ml) sugar

• Soak the sago in two cups (500 ml) water for at least 30 minutes or until soft, then drain. (Yields half cup soaked sago.)

• Bring the milk, cardamom and cinnamon stick to a gentle boil.
• Add the sago and allow to simmer over a low heat, stirring continuously until the sago becomes translucent and the milk thickens.
• Add the sweetener to taste.
• Remove the cinnamon stick before serving.

Sweet Potato Milk

Restore your energy with this very nutritious and filling beverage.

Preparation time: 15 minutes
Makes: 6 mugs

4 cups (1000 ml) milk
1 cinnamon stick (approx 5 cm)
1 large sweet potato (approx 460 g) boiled, peeled and mashed
Sugar or honey to taste

- Bring the milk and cinnamon stick to a gentle boil.
- Add the potato and sweetener.

Aniseed Tonic

Aniseed have a slight liquorice flavour and when added to milk makes a strengthening beverage.

Preparation time: 10 minutes
Makes: 4 mugs

4 cups (1000 ml) milk
1 tsp (5 ml) aniseed
4 tbs (60 ml) sugar or honey

- Bring the milk and aniseed to a gentle boil and allow to simmer for about 5 minutes.
- Stir in the sweetener and strain before serving.

GLOSSARY

Agar-agar (China grass) A seaweed extract used as a gelling agent.

Ajwain Small light brown seeds similar to caraway and cumin seeds. Generally used in snacks and some vegetable dishes.

Aniseed Small green and grey crescent shaped seeds that have a liquorice flavour.

Ayurveda A traditional Vedic system of medicine which is based on the idea of balance in bodily systems and uses diet, herbal treatment and yogic breathing.

Baking To cook by dry heat in an oven.

Basil An aromatic herb originating from India.

Basting Cooking food with liquid of oils or fats to prevent drying out.

Bay leaves A sweet-smelling leaf from the bay tree, often used in cooking.

Bhagavad Gita A Vedic scripture of India that was spoken 5000 years ago between Lord Krishna and his devotee Arjuna on the battlefield of Kuruksetra. Contains the essence of Vedic knowledge.

Blind baking Pre-baking in the oven for a short amount of time.

Braising To brown quickly in oil or fat at a high temperature.

Boiling A cooking method that requires cooking food in a liquid that has reached 100° C.

Camphor A sweet smelling crystalline substance obtained from the wood or bark of the camphor tree.

Cayenne pepper Dried red chili peppers ground into a fine powder.

Cardamom (Elachi) Small green pods that have the aromatic seeds inside. Open the pods before using. Can be ground into fine powder.

Carob An edible bean that grows on the carob tree. Has healthy properties and can be used to replace chocolate. Available at health stores.

Chili (Piment) A small hot-tasting pepper.

Cinnamon A sweet spice coming from the inner bark of the cinnamon tree.

Cloves (Laung) These are dried flower buds that look like small brown nails. They have a distinct spicy flavour and should be used sparingly.

Coriander seeds (Dhania seeds) Light brown and round seeds that can also be ground into fine powder. Adds a distinct flavour to foods so should be used in small quantities.

Cornflour Finely ground maize flour used for thickening sauces.

Cream cheese A soft rich cheese made from unskimmed milk and cream.

Cumin seeds (Jeera) Small light grey seeds that can be used whole or ground into a fine powder. Used mainly in vegetable dishes.

Curry leaves Highly aromatic dark green leaves that can be used in many curries.

Dhal A nutritious pea-like seed of a tropical shrub. Curry made from lentils or other pulses.
Mung dhal - comes from the mung bean. There are two types. Green mung is whole and round and split mung is small, yellow and rectangular.
Channa dhal - comes from the chickpea family. It is slightly large, round and yellow.
Toor dhal - pale, flat, large and yellow dhal. Also known as pigeon peas.

Deep-frying Frying in a large amount of oil.

GLOSSARY

Double boiler A container for holding hot water, in which sauces and other dishes are gently cooked or kept warm. Also known as a bain-marie.

Fennel seeds (Sauf) Similar to cumin seeds but used more in sweet dishes as it has a sweet liquorice flavour. Popular spice in Bengali curries where it is used in a preparation called five spices.

Feta cheese A Greek cheese made from sheep milk that is preserved in a salt solution.

Fenugreek seeds (Metti) Flat small brown seeds. Use with caution as it has a distinct bitter flavour.

Fresh coriander (Hara dhania) A slightly more pungent herb than parsley. A common ingredient in Indian cooking, generally used as a garnishing agent.

Ghee Clarified butter.

Garam masala A blend of cloves, cinnamon, cumin seeds, coriander seeds, cardamom and black pepper. Ground into fine powder.

Hing (Asafetida) An aromatic resin from the root of Ferula Asafetida. There are two varieties. The grey coarse hing should be grated before use and has a more pungent and acquired flavour than the yellow brand. Preferably use the yellow brand in small amounts to flavour food.

Kalonji seeds (Nigella) Small black seeds that have a peppery taste, also known as black onion seeds.

Masala A blend of ground spices. Also referred to as curry powder.

Mint (Pudina) A refreshing herb that has a strong tangy flavour. Commonly used in making chutneys, yoghurt drinks and fruit preparations.

Mustard seeds (Rai) Small black or yellow seeds that can be used whole or ground. When heated in oil they begin to splutter, releasing their flavour.

Nutmeg (Jaiphal) The seed from a tropical tree. The outer shell should be removed leaving the nut or mace, which should be grated or ground into fine powder.

Oregano A strong and sweet herb that is used in Italian preparations.

Panch Puran A mix of five spices. Generally cumin seeds, mustard seeds, fenugreek seeds, kalonji seeds and fennel.

Paprika A bright red powder that is made from sweet chili pepper pods that are not hot. Generally used as a garnish.

Parmesan A hard strong-flavoured cheese used grated on pasta dishes and soups.

Parsley A pleasant herb with a mild flavour. Generally used as a garnish.

Phyllo pastry A Greek pastry that is paper-thin. Can be purchased at most supermarkets.

Pressure-cooking Food cooked in an airtight pot in which food can be cooked quickly under steam pressure.

Rasam powder A blend of mustard seeds, cumin seeds, coriander seeds, black pepper and chilies that is ground into a fine powder. Used in a South Indian soup known as Rasam.

Rose essence Diluted essence of rose petals.

Rosemary An aromatic European shrub widely cultivated for its evergreen leaves. Has a similar flavour to pine. Should be used in small amounts.

Roux A cooked mixture of flour and fat used in the basis of sauces.

Saffron (Kesar) Known as the king of spices, saffron is the dried stigmas of the Saffron Crocus. This is a very expensive spice and adds royalty to a preparation. It has a delicate flavour and has a rich orange colour. Soak in a small amount of milk or water before using.

Sauté Frying vegetables lightly and quickly in a little oil or fat to ensure even cooking.

Semolina The large hard grains of wheat left after flour has been milled, used for making puddings and pasta.

Sesame seeds A small beige seed that has a nutty flavour and texture.

Simmering Cooking liquid over a low heat for a period of time.

Sprouts All beans and legumes can be sprouted. Once the seeds germinate they begin to sprout. Rich in nutrients, vitamin B and C, proteins and amino acids.

Starch flour (Potato flour) Wheat-free flour that has a strong binding property.

Stir-frying Tossing vegetables in a small amount of oil or fat in an open, wide and flat pan over a high heat.

Sunflower seeds A slightly large light grey seed that has a nutty flavour and texture.

Tamarind (Imli) These sour pods grow on trees in tropical countries. It has a brown pulp that should be soaked and strained from seeds before using.

Tookmaria seeds (Falooda seeds) Small black seeds that gel when added with water.

Turmeric (Heldi) A root similar to ginger that has a dark orange colour. Can be ground into powder.

Thyme A garden herb with white, pink, or red flowers that has a pleasant flavour.

Vedic literatures Ancient scriptures of India compiled 5000 years ago by Srila Vyasadeve, an incarnation of Lord Krishna.